DATING GUY

BREAKING DOWN BREAKUPS

A GUIDE THROUGH THE WINDING MAZE OF BREAKUPS

BREAKING DOWN BREAKUPS Copyright © 2020 to the author, Dating Guy. All rights reserved. Reproduction or redistribution of this book in any way, shape or form is forbidden and punishable by law. Any other sources are cited and used for educational purposes only. This material may not be reproduced, sold, recorded, photocopied, displayed publicly, stored in a retrieval system, or transmitted by any means possible, without written permission from the author.

To contact the author, email askdatingguy@gmail.com

Designed by Michael McInerney

Disclaimer: This book is for informational purposes only and does not render medical or psychological advice, opinion, diagnosis, treatment, or guarantee. The information provided should not be used for diagnosing or treating a health problem or disease. It is not a substitute for professional care. If you have or suspect you may have a medical or psychological problem, consult your appropriate health care provider. You are solely responsible for any action taken based on the information provided. Never disregard professional medical advice or delay in seeking it because of this book.

Introduction

I am under no illusion that you bought this book because of my charming personality or chiseled good looks. You are going through a breakup, and you need help. Culturally, breakups are mostly swept under the rug of mental health issues and merely dismissed as a "bummer". Those hurt by a breakup are told to simply "get over it" and reminded that there are plenty more fish in the sea. But the emotional impact a breakup can have on a person's life is highly underestimated by our society. In a flash, the life you built and the future you were planning for can be ripped away from you, your heart is smashed to pieces, and you feel like you're drowning in a sea of shock, rejection and pain. If the issues left behind remain unaddressed, this could have unintended negative consequences on your future relationships and your ability to trust and love again. But on the flip side, there is no greater catalyst for change than a breakup.

Since 2017, I have been helping people through breakups via email and through my Youtube channel. At the time of writing this, I have answered several thousand emails about breakups and dating issues. Meaning I have been exposed to almost every situation multiple times. I have seen what works and what does not work. And I assure you, that I write this book not just to create a little product to sell, but to compile as much of my experience and knowledge on the topic as I realistically can. I aim to make this as comprehensive as humanly possible, so that you, yes you, reading this right now, can directly download this information into the hard drive of your mind, which can in turn, influence better decision making from this moment on, with a deeper understanding of yourself, the situation you're specifically in, and breakups in general. Sometimes that requires staring the ugly truth in the face, being honest with yourself, not idealizing the past, and resisting some of your most primal overpowering instincts... but in the end, you will calm the current chaotic storm in your mind and find peace from a place of inner strength.

Whether you have just been dumped, or possibly ended the relationship yourself, or are experiencing an anxiety spiral, panicking, and trying to quickly find an instant solution to get your ex back, or you just want to understand your relationship better, heal and move on, I will do my best to take you through this process step-by-step. What I can't do... is lie to you. Right now, we are in a bad position. The relationship you had and commitment you likely wanted to maintain, has been terminated. That's a pretty awful day for anyone. I know, because I've been there. Unfortunately in dating, we are gambling with our own emotions, and no one gets out entirely unscathed.

But despite what your anxiety is telling you right now, you will heal from this, you will learn from this, and you will love again— whether that be with your ex or with somebody better.

Today you chose to put a stop to the madness, to silence your anxiety, and to try to educate yourself about love, relationships, dating, breakups and where you personally fit into this whole mess. And that's both something you should pat yourself on the back for, and a responsibility I take very seriously.

Contents

INTRODUCTION III

CHAPTER 1   **Understanding your Relationship** 5

CHAPTER 2   **The Dumper's Experience** 21

CHAPTER 3   **The Breakup** 34

CHAPTER 4   **The Immediate Aftermath** 51

CHAPTER 5   **Getting Yourself Back** 64

CHAPTER 6   **Take Your Ex Down from the Pedestal** 80

CHAPTER 7   **The Stages of No Contact** 98

CHAPTER 8   **The Exceptions and Situations of No Contact** 114

CHAPTER 9   **Social Media and Breakups** 131

CHAPTER 10   **Long-Distance Breakups** 146

CHAPTER 11   **Back In Contact** 167

CHAPTER 12   **Reconciliation** 201

FINAL REFLECTIONS 222

ACKNOWLEDGMENTS 226

NOTES 228

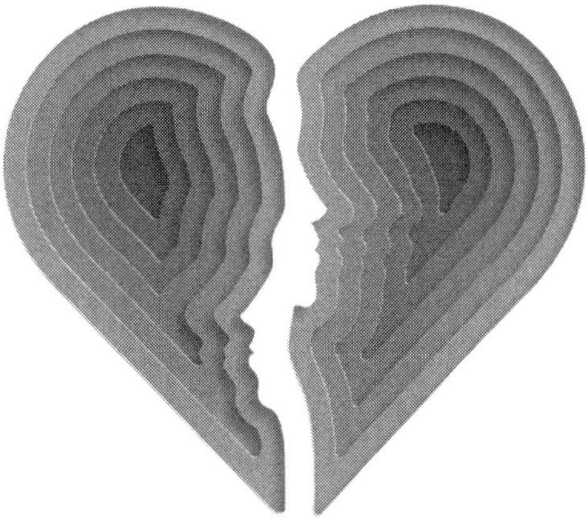

CHAPTER 1

Understanding Your Relationship

Some relationships are wonderful, but when they end we simply find a way to make peace and move on. Others are not so simple and feel as if they have touched our soul in a different way, whether we have known them for fifteen years or a couple of months. It's as if they have permanently captivated a part of you, and losing that person is like having a piece of your heart permanently removed. We feel naked, lost, alone, confused and robbed.

There are many reasons you may feel this way by the end of your relationship. Perhaps it is just simply the rejection (something we will delve further into in a later chapter). But perhaps it's something deeper. To be in a relationship with someone else is to partially manage and merge with another person's emotions and for the duration of your relationship, share a continuity of existence. But it is also a mirrored reflection of our relationship with ourselves; who we are at that point in our lives, what we knew, believed, and aspired to be.

People often struggle to describe what it is that they are truly attracted to within their partner. Sure, we can all describe physical features; great hair, killer smile, impressive butt. We could then justify our taste by their societal status, the money they make, the company they keep. But beyond the surface level, we start to hit personal preferences like interests, sense of humor, career, talents… and then we come to intangibles like smell, tone of voice, and a feeling of being "home". Ultimately, this all comes down to how the person makes you feel. But if you don't investigate the reason *why* they make you feel that way, then you may fall victim to ascribing romanticized mystical notions like "the one" to your partner, which never helps anything. How can you ever heal or accept that "the one" is gone? After all, they are *the* one right, not one of many, or just another one. *The. One.* Every word suggests singularity.

Most people will chalk it up to having a personal *type*. But then why is it that you can have several blonde-haired exes who work as lawyers but only care this much about one of them? Something has to be different, right?

Due to cultural influences like movies, novels, and music, human beings like to feel as if they are living in a story. As William Shakespeare put it, *'All the world's a stage, and all the men and women merely players; They have their exits and their entrances; And one man in his time plays many parts.'*[1]

In many respects, you are the protagonist of your own life. You make executive, defining decisions that shape your life. And those around us that we spend our time or love with, they are all co-stars in this giant play we call life. Family members are locked down permanent cast-members. Close friends are cast based on personal chemistry. Acquaintances are recurring characters. Co-workers come and go. But most people you pass on the street, sit near in restaurants, or wiggle past in bars, they are merely background extras.

The painful part about dating is that loving partners can fall into all of the above categories. A one night stand can be a cameo appearance, but a romantic partner will initially be cast due to personal chemistry, then they can feel as if they will be locked down as permanent cast members, but life may get in the way and they become an unexpected recurring character, and if things don't work out, they're written out of the show, and vanish into the out of focus background extras from which they were originally discovered.

Human beings like to feel as if they are living in a story. So why, out of all these possible auditioners and background extras, did you choose to cast your ex as your romantic co-star?

There are several questions to ask yourself that will help you understand your relationship with your partner in terms of selection and what they symbolize to you now that you are currently separated.

- What experiences had you already had romantically at this point?

- What did you expect the next year of your life to look like before meeting them?

- What is your biggest fear or weakness?

- What did you not know then, that due to your ex, you now know about yourself and relationships?

Let's take them one-by-one in a bit more depth. Remember that these questions may also be the key to understanding your relationship better from your ex's perspective too; why they are the way they are, why they chose to be with you, and how/why they chose to leave.

What experiences had you already had romantically at this point?

This is a critically important question to understand the story that you were currently living in at the time you met your partner. Whether you like to think so or not, you were living in a story. Your romantic history up until this point does shape your worldview and make you more susceptible, available, or attracted to certain types of partners. These partners then become something more than just people. They become an idea to you.

Examples:

- Perhaps you had limited experience romantically and this person was your first real romantic connection, so this person symbolizes your introduction to the formerly unknown world of powerful romantic connections.

- Perhaps you had given up on love due to a string of failed relationships or "almost-relationships" and now this partner symbolizes the last throw of the dice so you feel as if you need them or will be alone forever.

- Perhaps you had a controlling or abusive partner(s) in the past, and this relationship now symbolizes you breaking free from your previous traumatic relationship, and without it, you feel as if you will fall back into that dark pattern.

- Perhaps you had low self-esteem or ugly-duckling syndrome due to childhood bullying, and this partner was the most physically attractive person you've ever been with, so now they symbolize the idea of you overcoming the childhood bullies and having something of a "trophy" (aka. A symbol) next to you to prove your past tormentors or past self wrong.

- Perhaps your parents divorced when you were young, and on some level this caused you to lose faith in long-term love. Now that you have seen how bad things can get, you either bolt at the first sign of trouble within a relationship to protect yourself from experiencing the same pain you witnessed your parents go through. Or no matter how bad a relationship gets, you never let go, as your partner now symbolizes you re-enacting and resolving your parents' breakup from your childhood.

What did you expect the next year of your life to look like before meeting them?

We all tend to plan our futures, whether it be in the short, medium or long term. Every plan we make for our futures, on some level, delivers us a specific set of anxieties and obstacles to overcome. Each day comes with a set of short-term expectations and goals. Some as pressurized as organizing a major event, and some as minor as picking a nice place to go for lunch. Either way, these short-term goals force us to go out into the world and act. Our bodies and minds are focused on the main task at hand. But our subconscious is processing these current actions, alongside your medium and long term goals. These can all merge together in your subconscious, crossing lines and causing confusing emotions to surface at inopportune moments. This is often why you may find yourself achieving plenty of short-term goals but feeling empty or dissatisfied, because perhaps that does not benefit your medium or long term goals, giving you a feeling of futility and lack of direction.

On some level, we are all always lost and searching for something that may resolve these feelings of uncertainty. This is why if you examine who you were and what you expected to happen next, you can gain a clear insight into what you needed at the time.

Examples:

- Perhaps you had just moved to a new city/country and did not know anyone as intimately as your friends and family back home. You expected the next year of your life to look a little lonely, perhaps intimidating and unclear. You needed someone to rely on, to explore with, to feel safe with. And you were highly susceptible to becoming very attached and dependent on this person, as they now symbolize a bright future in this city with a lot more clarity, as well as helping to settle a lot of anxiety you had before arriving because now everything is falling into place. So they symbolize the stabilizing of the unstable and a big risk paying off, which helps you to trust yourself to take more risks, which is always needed to survive in a new city.

- Perhaps you were suffering from depression and struggled to even see a future. But then this person brought you out of your shell and you began to create future plans together. Your ex-partner now symbolizes a possible bright future and without them, you feel as if you revert back to your previous self.

- Perhaps you were chaotically busy at work and had written off the next few years as a time to hunker down and put time into your career without much of a social life. Your day-to-day routine had become monotonous. But then you met your ex and they made your life more exciting and unpredictable. Without them, your life feels dull and joyless as you relied on them too much to make you happy in your free time outside the office.

- Perhaps you have kids and have no plans to date as you worry about how you can seamlessly blend a new romantic partner into a domesticated world of responsibilities and child-rearing. You then meet a partner that completely proves you wrong and your anxiety about life as a single parent is not only quashed but surpassed. Without them, you have a fear that your life will regress back to being more isolated and less satisfying.

What is your biggest fear or weakness?

We all have insecurities and fears. Ask yourself, on a deeper emotional level, what is your biggest fear? The answer is not spiders or heights, it's something deeper than that. Those fears guide your decision making. We all do this in a variety of ways. If you fear being poor, you work extra hard to be financially comfortable. If you fear becoming sick, you carry hand sanitizer. Additionally, you may start to become attracted to people that possess the very strength that you lack. This makes your mind feel as if it's growing and resolving problems with this person.

Examples:

- All your friends are settling down, but you are single and always wanted to travel, but don't have the time or anyone to go with. Then you meet your partner. Maybe they are foreign and just visiting your country, so they symbolize a possible escape from your immediate surroundings. Or they can work from anywhere, so they open up a door to more travel opportunities for you. Or perhaps they are an unemployed vagabond, but their reckless lust for life appeals to you because they conquer your personal fears regularly like it's nothing at all. This makes you feel stronger with them.

- You have a fear of public speaking, but then you meet your charismatic partner who works as a performer. Their acceptance of you makes you feel part of a world you would otherwise have no access to. This makes you develop more confidence in an area you always felt insecure.

- You struggle to make major decisions or are at a crossroads in life and have no idea what to do next. Then you meet your partner, who has a very specific and clear path that they follow. Their strength gives you strength, and you either choose to follow their path, or they help you find a path of your own. Without them, you feel directionless or as if all the decisions you made while you were with them no longer make sense.

- You have addiction problems. You find yourself unable to attend certain social events because you can no longer enjoy them. Then you meet your partner who happens to live a naturally healthy lifestyle so doesn't go to those kinds of events anyway. You develop a whole new lease on life with them and you now symbolize them with conquering your addiction and still finding life fulfilling.

- Maybe you were financially inexperienced and your partner was successful and had a flashy lifestyle. They helped you build yourself up, become financially independent and get a job that satisfies you. Without them, you feel lost and scared you may revert back to your previous self.

What did you not know then, that due to your ex, you now know about yourself and relationships?

Sometimes we come out of a relationship feeling as if we have been stripped of a lot of our own personality and power. We may then fear that without that person by our side we will never get to experience the same worldview or activities anymore, as we now symbolize that person with unlocking a part of our own personality that we did not know we had. All relationships gift us new experiences and teach us something about ourselves, but sometimes we learn the wrong lessons from the right experience. Instead of this lesson being learned and building our character, we do not take a step forward, but instead, look backwards, or even begin to spin in circles. Sometimes you have to be harsh and ask what this relationship taught you about love and yourself? This way you can establish that you have already learned the lesson and do not need to repeat the same pattern again.

Examples:

- You have always been very needy and anxious in relationships and it has pushed a lot of your previous partners away over time, but your latest partner is fiercely independent and highly avoidant. You may admire this about them because it's a quality you lack. But now that your relationship is over, you feel you must either seek an even more avoidant partner, or get this most recent partner back, because by getting them back you can prove to yourself that you can win over even the most highly avoidant partners, and thus, resolve your feelings of inadequacy from previous breakups and end the cycle on a cathartic "win".

- Let's say you are young and due to a strict upbringing you have never really experienced much of a party lifestyle. Then you meet your partner, who is wild and somewhat self-destructive. They teach you how to loosen up, enjoy the present tense more, and stop worrying so much about consequences. This causes you to discover a fresh side to your personality. They now symbolize you exploring other ways of life, rebelling against your parents' upbringing, and meeting a lot more people than you ever have before. But rather than learning that you are a lot freer than you previously told yourself, you only feel safe exploring your adventurous side within the confines of another similar relationship.

- Maybe you tried a long-distance relationship for the first time. You made big promises to yourself based on romantic ideals. Perhaps believing that this is the ultimate test of true love. But then it doesn't work out, and you learn that long-distance relationships do not work long-term. But you now symbolize your partner with this harsh lesson, and on some level fear that you could have succeeded had you played it differently. You then try to recreate that cycle with another long-distance relationship, and another, until you eventually make it work and resolve this feeling that you are a failure, due to your guilt of breaking that initial promise to yourself, as this will prove you *are* worthy of true love.

- Or it could be that you are disappointed with your performance within the relationship. Maybe you acted needy, insecure and desperate, which is totally unlike you. You then learned not to do that from this breakup but now feel as if you need your partner back to prove to them that you are better than the version of you they saw, especially towards the end of your relationship together. Without that validation, you will not feel capable of moving on.

Sometimes the simplest way of understanding what you're attracted to is to examine your own dating history. Typically when we think of our exes, we distinguish them by their differences; different jobs, different hair color, different nationalities. But you likely gain a lot more insight into what you are really looking for by observing the similarities. We often tell ourselves a flattering story about the qualities we are looking for in a partner because it makes us feel good. Yet our relationship history often does not reflect that. If you find yourself in a string of failed relationships, then it may be time to investigate what type of partner you keep attracting and why you are subconsciously seeking these traits.

On separate pieces of paper, write out lists and answers to the following questions:

1. What type of partner do I think I am looking for?

2. What type of partner do I keep finding?

Place those two pieces of paper down in order. Now that you have established that baseline, let's add extra layers and investigate why you are subconsciously seeking that type of partner...

- Why would I be attracted to the qualities from list 2 in a partner?

- Do I admire this quality because I lack it or share it?

- What is my earliest memory of admiring this quality?

- Why is that memory important to me?

Place these pieces of paper below the previous two. These lists map out the layers of you; from who you think you are, to who you actually are, to what your experiences have taught you to seek. If there is a clear difference between list 1 and 2, then you are expecting to arrive at a different destination than your subconscious has put into the GPS.

There are many reasons why you chose your ex in the first place that goes beyond the surface level of what they look like. Yes, looks may be a part of your particular selection too, let's not pretend physical attraction doesn't play a role, it does. But who you were when you met them is a bigger indicator of what you needed at the time and this helps you to understand what they provided. Just like you were living in a story when you first met them, that story evolved and changed in tandem with them, and now you are currently living in another story.

The current story in your head is likely:

- You don't know what you got till it's gone.

Or it could be:

- I fucked up and now my life is ruined

- Without that person I am nothing

- They were right to leave me

But that story itself will evolve and change as your mindset evolves and changes. Whether you like to think so or not, by the end of this book you are not going to feel the same way about your breakup. We should both be able to agree that this can only be a good thing because this current anxious and painful state you are in right now, is not ideal and you deserve better than this.

Now that you have examined your relationship history and asked yourself some tough questions, you have a deeper understanding of what your ex-partner provided for you internally. It is important to identify that although everyone is unique and your ex may just be absolutely amazing— *like seriously, Oh my God, wow*. But more than likely, your selection of this person and their selection of you, has a lot more to do with who you both were at the time, what you expected your life to be like, and what you both needed. Romantic relationships are invaluable and add a certain flavor to our lives. It can often feel like the difference between seeing in black and white and seeing in color. Or the difference between just hearing noise and hearing music. But the reason we hold these unique relationships so dearly is because they are often a reflection of our relationship with ourselves. What and who you choose to attach yourself to, is symbolic of what you *believe* is essential for your happiness. But that does not necessarily make it so. As, you guessed it, that's just a story you're telling yourself.

CHAPTER 2

The Dumper's Experience

Similarly to how you subconsciously selected your ex, they chose you. Through something as traumatic and painful as a breakup, we can often lose sight of the fact that the person who ended the relationship was also an equal participant within it. The only real currency we have is time. It's finite, and there is no greater compliment than someone choosing to spend their limited time on this planet, with you. Never forget that they wanted this too, likely sharing your exact feelings along the way, and when your romance initially blossomed they had nothing but the best of intentions, and like you, found themselves incapable of turning back, protecting themselves, or resisting. Just like you feel as if they completed you, you completed them.

But no one gets out of a relationship or through a breakup unscathed. While the one who is rejected suffers far more of a shock and blow to their self-esteem, the one who chooses to end it suffers from self-doubt, confusion, and guilt.

A lot of the time in breakups, the dumpee will argue with the dumper, reminding them of all the good times they shared together. This is because the dumpee feels as if this must be a totally spontaneous decision for the dumper. But sadly, when you invoke romantic memories with your partner as evidence of your enduring love, you're shocked to find that they do not seem phased by this. It can come across as cold, heartless and almost sociopathic. How does this person who has been in love with me for months or years not share in the joy of *this* or *that* romantic memory? And the answer is simple. They have already thought about this before making their decision. You are being reactive in the moment of the breakup, assuming that this is as fresh for them as it is for you. But sadly it's not the case. Dumpers don't suddenly have their relationship stripped from them, so they don't feel their world crumble as if nothing makes sense. But rather, their relationship slips away from them and they find themselves confused by their own fading love. It's as if an undercurrent of doubt shivers through their body, but rather than passing, it sits and grows like a tumor.

Now, of course, breakups can be spontaneous (especially with younger people, or) in the heat of an argument. The idea of breaking up can even be used as a negotiation tactic within the relationship; either to manipulate or just as simple hyperbole. As if you or your partner are subtextually communicating, "*I care more about this than you and I'm willing to prove it by walking away forever*" or just using it as hyperbole like, "*I'd rather never eat again than cook dinner tonight*". These incidents are often what is called a "fake breakup". Essentially that means that it was spontaneous and done to prove a point more than it was ever to actually cut ties with one another. The problem with this is that over time it can weaken your relationship and subconsciously plant the idea in both of your minds that ending the relationship is the only way to solve a problem, which then, over time, becomes the only logical decision because all recurring problems cannot be resolved that way.

But anyway, for most dumpers, they begin to experience the relationship killer known as doubt. The reasons vary, it could be external stresses, no time together, a complacent sex life, repetition and mundanity, identifying internal incompatibilities, arguments, or just a sudden feeling as if from nowhere that this doesn't suit them any longer. The two tentpole reasons for breaking up are: **a loss of attraction** *or* **not seeing a future with you**. There are lots of smaller sub-categories we will cover in a later chapter, but almost every reason can be divided into these two categories. And this is where the dumper's doubt begins. A seed is planted in their mind that maybe this relationship is not for them.

They're not stupid so they won't just have some doubt and instantly break up with you. It usually festers over a few weeks or even months in some long term cases. And they spend this time trying their best to ignore that thought, that feeling, because it's not what they want. Remember that they chose to be in this relationship too. And that is often where they start... they reflect on the start of your romance.

They cycle through all the positive memories you have together trying to use it as evidence to convince themselves to stay and figure it out (hence why you invoking these later feels futile to them). This can help them bat away initial concerns because they remind themselves about what worked in the beginning and how they fell in love. But this can backfire over time. If they start to think about what works, they then may start comparing their current feeling to the past. This highlights the gulf between what you both *were* at the idealistic start and what you both *are* now. If problems repeat and persist, they can then grow tired of having to think back all the time, rather than having fresh examples in front of them. They can feel as if they are now using the fumes of the past to feed their present tense.

They may also think back to who they were when they met you (as we discussed in Chapter One), what they expected their future to look like, and what they needed at the time, and start realizing that this relationship isn't going in the direction they expected it to. Or even that their own life isn't going in the direction they hoped it would, and this gets projected onto the relationship.

Either way, they don't feel it all the time, but they just have doubts about staying and if this is right for them anymore. Remember that they had a whole life and set of expectations before meeting you. This is often why exes regress after breakups. They are reverting back to who they were before they started the relationship as that is their last known state of independence.

Rather than pull the plug right away, they often try to mimic themselves in the relationship for a little while, assuming this must just be a weird phase. They'll smile, say I love you, go on dates... and it feels a little better, but it's not working. That doubtful gut instinct just lingers. Something is wrong. It could be that you are just arguing and there really is nothing worth fighting for anymore. But more often, it's an existential crisis that they are just in the wrong place and unsure where the right place even is or what their life should look like. It's the same kind of existential crisis you may have lying in bed awake one night wondering about your career. *Am I on the right path? How long should I stay stuck in this job? Will it get better? Am I reaching my potential? Should I quit? Should I run away to an exotic island? Is this it?*

So now if faking it isn't working, they decide some time apart may help. So they pull away more. This is often what can be called a 'Slow Fade' by dumpees in hindsight.

Where you suspect something is wrong but don't know how to fix it. Rather than having your partner just break up with you, they start slowly fading out of your life. They respond to texts less, they're less available, and seem to be prioritizing other people, activities and desires. Subconsciously, they are starting to break up with you, but they don't really realize it yet. They are just taking time away to figure things out for themselves. But by doing so they are sampling out what life is like outside of the relationship. Adjusting to it. And on some level, preparing the dumpee for a breakup so that it does not shock them. Psychologically, dumpers do not do this to be cold. As I said, they may do it because they are genuinely trying to make it work. But they also do it because on some level they think if you are less used to having them around, then you won't be so upset if the relationship ends. And a small percentage will be trying to pull away until you end the relationship for them because they don't have the courage to hurt you to your face.

Either way, whatever reaction they hoped for, they often get the exact opposite. The dumpee feels it happen and rather than seeing it as a sign that maybe things are not working, each day becomes more tragic. It's as if they can see and touch their partner but they feel they are mentally existing somewhere else. So while the dumper pulls away— their partner seems to be coming closer, smothering them. This is because the dumpee's anxiety is spiked and they start having fight or flight impulses, thinking *"I'm not letting this relationship die without a fight*", which is very noble, but ironically is the exact opposite of what the dumper wants in that moment.

This is when dumpees start to show more and more interest. Their logic being that if the dumper is showing 20% interest, then if the dumpee simply shows 180% interest then you are both still at the appropriate combined 200%, so nothing is wrong. Unfortunately, this only highlights the gulf between both of you. The dumper can now see an example of what love should look like and how interested they would need to be to stay in this relationship, and they can't even muster half of that. So it helps them to cement in their decision that this just won't work. In these moments, it's impossible to see, but a reality is that both people are currently not compatible anymore as their desires and needs are totally different.

Now the dumper pulls away even more and starts to act cold, so they can isolate themselves and figure out; *what the hell is wrong with me*? They think about the good times, the connection, the story they told themselves up until now about why you both belong together. But the feeling can't be shaken. And they begin to doubt themselves and their own capacity for love and what must be missing in them and how all of this must be their fault.

Throughout all of this, they feel mentally isolated, because they've tried acting, they've tried pulling away, but no matter what they do, there is just this feeling that this isn't working and now that they've started to see more evidence coming out of the dumpee's behavior, they then conclude this can't continue.

In order to not feel isolated anymore, they often choose to consult with a friend. At this moment they just need someone they can confide in, as they need to figure out what they feel and they're getting nowhere by themselves, and they fear if they tell their partner it could be irreparable and they aren't sure what they even want yet. Their friend will likely encourage them to do what they think is right for them, like any friend would. This helps the dumper make a decision, and usually bolstered by that support, they gravitate closer to the riskier decision (breaking up).

But there is still a lot of uncertainty. *What if it's the wrong choice? Where did this feeling come from? Can't I get over this?*

Either way, as you know, in the end, they decided that they wanted to break up. And here we are.

The reason I want you to understand what the dumper experience is like is because if we simply dismiss our ex as "crazy" or "heartless" then we gain no understanding of their reasoning or feelings. And if you don't know what you're actually up against then you will likely pursue fixing the problem in a biased way that resolves your own anxiety, but ignores their actual needs. They are living in a story too and they have their own version of your break-up. Their version is emotional but it is also reasonable and does not paint them in a particularly positive light. So if we want to turn the tables, we cannot assume they made this decision with malice. They likely did it because as much as it hurts you, they suspect you will both be better off thanks to their decision in the long run. They view their decision as something that needed to happen. Why? Because they made it happen and most people do not think of themselves as foolish idiots who make idiotic mistakes.

But now that we understand what a lot of dumpers experience before breaking up, let's examine some of the factors that may contribute to them feeling this way that has nothing to do with you.

Age. As we are all the lead characters in our own lives, our level of experience shapes how we make decisions. The human brain keeps growing and developing until the age of 25. But aside from our own maturity, our age is often indicative of what stage we are at in our lives... or worse, what stage we expected ourselves to be at, but aren't yet.

For example, let's say that by 30 you wanted to be a successful singer, but you're not. This type of identity crisis can cause you to lose trust in your own decision making, as the decisions that have lead you up until this point did not lead you to your targeted destination. So you suspect perhaps you need to push away in a new direction, out of your comfort zone. You also may choose to not blame yourself (as blaming yourself can often involve painful introspection) and instead blame those around you. Therefore you or your relationship becomes the perfect scapegoat.

Others may reach a certain age and think, *"Is this it? Is this what I envisioned for myself when I was a child?"* Or if you have been together for years with your ex-partner and they have either planned to move in with you or get married or have kids (a major next step in your relationship), but then they suddenly get cold feet. They are scared of the level of responsibility and risk that awaits, so they regress and decide they would rather have fun, maybe go traveling, or something far less serious and responsible. Some will call this a mid-life crisis or a quarter-life crisis. Others will call it 'Cold Feet' or 'Grass is Always Greener Syndrome'. This is, unfortunately, all part of human nature and has far more to do with them than you.

Up until the age of 30, everything is up in the air and dating, relationships and breakups can be a total minefield because people are in the process of building their prospective lives. They are told to have fun and experience everything, but also to make good choices that will build a bright future for themselves, and while all of this is going on, they should ideally find the perfect partner too and maybe settle down. Life is both simple and very complicated, and each person's path is different from the other. Sometimes that's liberating and sometimes it's isolating.

Through answering thousands of emails about breakups and through my own experience, I've noticed that a lot of the time people end relationships at certain milestones in their twenties. Typically around 18, 22, 26, and 30. But why? What's the motivation? It's usually centered around radical change, or due to an inner conflict due to a lack of change.

Examples:

- ***18*** - *"Oh my God— I am going to college— I want to be free and independent to figure out who I am and adapt to my new life"*

- ***22*** - *"Oh my God— College is over and the real world awaits— I want to be free and independent to figure out who I am and adapt to my new life"*

- ***26*** - *"Okay, I have figured out what I do and don't want and if I am going to succeed I need to steer in that direction, but I need to be alone to do so"*

- ***30*** - *"Okay, I know myself, this isn't quite right for me… but I think I know what is now"*

Other factors that may contribute to your breakup that have nothing to do with you are; long-distance, work stress, and mental health. Romantic relationships involve two flawed human beings trying to balance their own expectations of romance, their individual plans for the future, their career, their friends' personal problems, their family's personal problems, all while enjoying the present moment and being a responsible, loyal partner. When unexpected external factors come into play, or the pressure is dialed up on existing obligations, it becomes harder to balance everything, and sometimes harsh decisions need to be made. Dumpers can sometimes feel as if they are so overwhelmed with external obligations that are outside of their control, that they need to cut out unnecessary additional pressures like romantic relationships because, at the time, they can see no other way forward.

There is also the ugly possibility that your ex has either physically cheated on you or emotionally cheated on you by starting to talk with someone else, who is tempting them away from the relationship. But normally in order for that to have happened, the above wheels are already in motion. The cheating is a symptom, not the cause. Most people will naturally assume that their ex has cheated on them after a breakup, but it is not normally the case. The reason we suspect this is because we know our ex as a romantic, sexual being, and we know that they have the capacity for love. So if they no longer want to do that with us, we assume they must instantly filling that void with someone else. It's our greatest fear, and in the moment you are being broken up with, it seems like things can't get any worse, so you figure why not make it a full house, and assume they are cheating too.

It's important to remember that at the time of breaking up, the dumper is not fully certain of their decision, feels tremendous guilt for hurting you, and is highly confused about their own capacity for love. They view themselves as somewhat heartless and can see that they are a disappointment to you. They are also unsure what comes next for them. But at the time they make the decision, they have had these feelings for some time already, and when they finally muster the courage to start the breakup, they see no way back. Which brings us to our next chapter: The Breakup itself.

CHAPTER 3

The Breakup

Breakups are traumatizing for both parties involved. The dumper goes into the experience highly cautious, knowing they are about to set an emotional bomb off. They are expecting pushback, anger, and sadness. Whereas the dumpee typically feels blindsided (no matter how much they saw it coming) and spirals into a state of panic. There are a few different ways in which the dumper may decide to break up. The method chosen will tell you something about the dumper; how they deal with conflict, their empathy level, their anxiety level, how certain they are, or their attachment style.

- *Cold and clinical:* This is often a shock to the dumpee because the one they love is suddenly behaving like a stone-cold killer. They are giving you zero hope and just brutally sticking to the fact that it is over. They do not do this because they want to hurt you. In reality, it's that they think this will cause both of you the least pain, the least negotiation, and that you will not hold onto false hope. So although it may feel the opposite way, their motivation is to help you in the long run by hurting you in the short term.

- ***Exceptionally Kind:*** The dumper takes full responsibility for the breakup and assures the dumpee they did nothing wrong. But by trying to defuse all tension and anger, the dumpee is left behind with more confusion as to why it won't work between you. They think that, *'if you're such a fan of me, then really we should be together,'* and they hold onto hope, typically trying to force the dumper to say something nasty so they can have something negative to hold onto.

- ***Unbearably uncertain:*** All dumpers are uncertain, but sometimes they are so uncertain that they drive a conversation towards a breakup without wanting to say it themselves. Their behavior will exhibit a lot of distance and a lack of communication. They don't know what to say. If you ask them if they want to break up, they will say 'no' but then not come up with any solutions. Instead, they will repeat the same doubts over and over in the hopes that you will choose to end it on their behalf. This is cruel because the dumpee winds up initially ending a relationship that they want to continue, just to spare the dumper the official responsibility. Almost like having to shoot yourself to save the other person the trauma of taking a human life. Once you suggest breaking up— they agree and become resolute in that decision because it has finally been said. They realize this is what they really need. The dumpee, on the other hand, is totally bewildered, as once the dumper confirms they now want to end it, the dumpee realizes they suggested something they don't even want, so they flip and try to talk them out of it. They then cannot understand how the dumper goes from being uncertain to suddenly cemented in their position in just a few minutes. These breakups tend to go on for a long time and leave the dumpee even more confused because the dumper wanted to avoid conflict at all costs.

- **The Spontaneous Argument:** The dumper decides that they don't think this relationship is working, but they don't want to make it seem like it's something they no longer want for no good reason. So they start arguments and disagree with you more. The dumpee is often confused and can feel their partner pull away, but usually chalks it up to a bad mood. When the dumper does successfully trigger an argument, they then use this as a springboard into a breakup so that everyone can feel it was a somewhat spontaneous decision. This leaves the dumper confused and expecting that things will just calm down as it appears to be a "fake breakup".

- **The Slow Fade**: The dumper starts to suspect

this relationship is not for them anymore. Rather than confront the issue and try to fix it, they begin to pull away. They think they are being very subtle, but the dumpee notices them pull away and starts to try to subconsciously fix the situation by coming closer. This causes the dumper to pull further away, being less responsive to all forms of contact. The dumper hopes that this will slowly detach both parties from the intense emotions of the breakup, as you are both used to spending less time together. It also makes it more difficult for the dumpee to argue against because they can't say it came out of nowhere. This sounds reasonable on paper, but after a strong connection has been formed, it feels more like a slow death to the dumpee.

- **The Big Discussion**: Sometimes dumpers don't know they are going to break up yet, but instead decide they have to have a "big discussion", in which they are going to air all of their thoughts and feelings. If the dumpee gets defensive or shuts down, this will spiral into an argument resulting in a breakup. If the dumpee participates, maybe they work things out. But more often than not, the dumper wants to take the dumpee on a journey through their problems, and their thoughts and feelings on said problems, so that they can help them come to the only conclusion they were ever going to come to… that they want to break up.

The aim of this can be to help the dumpee see that the relationship is not working and feel as if it is somewhat mutual.

- ***The Quick Text***: Breakup conversations are tough. Most dumpers fear disappointing the one they care about, they fear seeing that look of sadness or disappointment in their eyes, and on some level, they may also know that their reasons are flimsy and may not stand up to scrutiny in a breakup debate… so they decide it's simplest for everyone if they just send a quick text. A drive-by breakup. Dumpers who do this are somewhat matter-of-fact about it. They think that if it is going to happen, then the format doesn't really matter. Dumpees who are abandoned via text usually feel that it's a sign of disrespect and like they meant nothing to the dumper.

- ***Ghosting:*** Some dumpers are total cowards. They hate conflict and letting people down. They usually have a prolific dating history and find breakup conversations a bit too emotionally taxing and feel they have had one too many. They start the slow fade but then decide not to even confront it. They just disappear. Maybe they block you or just stop answering texts or calls, but either way, they're gone. The dumpee is left behind confused as to what they did wrong and it triggers an anxiety spiral about why they are not worthy of a simple goodbye.

Through answering thousands of emails I can assure you that there is no perfect way to break up with someone. Often people who have been broken up with by text will insist that they would feel "totally fine" had it been done in person. For those who break up face-to-face, they will feel they would have been "totally fine" had the dumper just said something a little differently. However, it's rarely the methodology or the specific words used that cause such dissatisfaction... it's the decision itself that the dumpees take real issue with. This is why these processes are so traumatizing for both people involved. No matter the method or approach, the dumpee is going to be upset. The future you have both been envisioning, and the present lifestyle you have both been simultaneously experiencing, is suddenly gone. The world no longer really makes sense to the dumpee and they can lose trust in themselves and others for some time. The dumper leaves a breakup feeling raw and exposed as a fraud. They enter a new world of uncertainty that they now feel a responsibility for. So while the dumpee feels hopeless, unattractive, and lost, the dumper feels uncertain and lost, but with a lot of pressure to prove this was the right decision.

Decoding the Reasons Given For Breaking Up:

After a breakup, the dumpee feels an immediate rush to try to get their ex back. They recycle over the breakup conversation playing out scenarios of what they could have done or said differently. No matter what was said in the breakup, they start trying to figure out the "real truth" behind the breakup. They do this as a way of trying to solve the problem. If they think through every possibility then they can come up with the perfect strategy to undo the decision. This is of course just part of the anxiety spiral of any loss. The dumpee does not realize it yet, but they are grieving, and currently experiencing both the denial and bargaining stage at the same time (but we will cover that more in a later chapter).

Whatever reasons were given in your specific breakup, they likely fall under one of (or both of) these two key tentpole reasons; *a loss of attraction or not seeing a future with you*. Sometimes it can be both but generally all reasons given fall under these two categories. Not sure which one you fall under? Let's figure it out now.

A Loss of Attraction:

- "You are smothering me"

- "I am too busy to give you what you need"

- "You don't look after yourself anymore"

- "We argue too much"

- "Our sex life is dead"

- "We never do anything, we stay in too much"

- "You aren't the same since you lost your job"

- "I've met someone else"

- "You're not who I thought you were"

Not Seeing a Future with You:

- "We are too different"

- "We don't have the same interests anymore. We've grown apart"

- "We can't communicate properly"

- "You cheated on me and the trust is broken"

- "We want different things (marriage, kids, house, career, lifestyle)"

- "We don't live in the same city/country and I can't keep pretending we do"

- "You are not financially responsible enough to build a future with"

- "It's too complicated and I'm tired of it"

What is the Story of Your Breakup?

If you're reading this because you want to get your ex back, the patterns I have noticed is that certain stories cause dumpers to revisit the idea of reconciliation more than others. This is why it's important to try to understand '**The Story of the Breakup**' from your ex's perspective. This means that you can picture your ex explaining to their friends and family why you are both no longer together. Now at first, both parties involved typically can't see the woods for the trees because they are too close to it to really understand it. It was an emotional decision. But imagine the difference from day one, to day 60, and then 6 months. The story of your breakup tends to evolve and reveal itself properly. As if you are looking at an impressionist painting and each month you take another step back until you both now see the full picture.

An example could be that on your first impression you'll think the story is: "We *broke up because we argue about stupid stuff all the time*". Then that might evolve into the second impression: "We *have very different interests*". And then a final impression would be: "We're *not compatible long-term because we want different things*". By understanding your relationship and your breakup, you can then determine the likelihood that they will or won't reconsider over time. The difficulty lies in being brutally honest with yourself and not allowing your bias to get in the way. This is about what you think *is* true, not what you wish were true. To help you out, let's dive a little deeper with examples:

- If a dumper thinks you are ***internally incompatible***; meaning they think you have totally different interests, communication styles, different hopes for the future, different religions/cultures... then they are less likely to reconsider because these are internal differences that are integral to who you both are as individuals. To change that would be to change the person fundamentally and that in itself would require unnecessary effort that sucks the romance out of the relationship. Even though they may miss you and wonder about you, they will mentally have a logical hesitation about reconnecting because they know that this fundamental difference either will not or should not change.

- If a dumper thinks you have ***unfinished business***; meaning that your relationship was unfairly cut short, then they are more likely to wonder about that relationship and what could have been. Typically unfinished business is left behind when external factors get in the way of your relationship. This could be work stress, family problems, health issues, not being emotionally ready for a relationship, or long distance/visa problems being in play. If other factors got in the way of your romance, then the dumper will wonder if those issues are still a factor as time goes by. Unfinished business leaves behind a question mark. An itch that needs to be scratched. It's as though you aren't an "ex", but an "incomplete".

- Similarly, if the dumper feels that the story of your breakup is that **the timing was just wrong,** then time is forever changing, and they are more likely to occasionally fantasize that perhaps now the timing is right. This could happen when they go on a bad date or find themselves unhappy in their next relationship. They start to wonder about you and your story of poor timing and wondering how things have changed for you now. This is where your own personal growth is vitally important. It could be that at the time you broke up either your ex or you had to focus on your studies or work, that there were personal health issues altering either their behavior or yours, or long distance was in play but now it isn't, or that you were unemployed but now you have your shit together, or that you were anxious, depressed or stressed, but now appear active, attractive and content. If the timing was wrong, and they were overwhelmed with stress, or they lost attraction for you because of what you were doing, more than who you were, then they are more likely to reconsider in the future when those issues are resolved.

- If the dumper has secretly developed feelings for someone else, and either physically or emotionally cheats, and then **monkey branches** to that new person, then they are less likely to return. Why?

Firstly because they have experienced themselves slowly but surely betraying your trust. These betrayals may have made them feel guilty but they ultimately continued until they enjoyed the fruits of their labor with a new romantic partner. Even if their next monkey branch relationship fails, they are less likely to return as the story of your breakup is that they already valued you too little and thought there was someone or something better for them out there. So if this new person isn't the answer, then they tend not to think the person who came before them was either, and instead continue to look to the future.

- If the dumper feels that in hindsight they simply got **cold feet** at a scary upcoming change then time apart may make them realize that the grass is not always greener on the other side of the fence and they can then tell themselves the story that they were just not thinking clearly. Typically dumpers experiencing this will back out because something big is about to change that scares them. Maybe they just turned 30, or left college, or started a new job, or you're engaged or all your friends are getting engaged, or you're about to move in together. Either way, you can expect to hear phrases like, *"I'm not ready for this"* or *"I really need to focus on getting my career in order"* or *"we want different things"*, and that just happens to coincide with a major change or turning point in either their life or your relationship together.

- A different way of phrasing the same question is simply: *Did they break up with you or the situation?*

Common Breakup Mistakes:

When the breakup conversation does take place, whether they felt it coming or it was a total shock, the dumpee typically spirals into anxiety and cycles through a series of strategies in order to convince the dumper not to pull the plug. While their arguments can be compelling, they often don't change the dumper's mind in the end.

The most common mistakes are:

- ***Logic Trap***: The dumpee is an excellent debater and has realized that there is a hole in the dumper's reasoning. They then use logic to try to convince them to stay, as if by pointing out how irrational they are being will somehow convince them not to feel the way they do. The dumpee usually presents these arguments as if the dumper physically has no choice to leave unless they can pass the logic test.

- ***Using the Past Against Them:*** The dumpee will invoke romantic memories and refuse to accept that things have changed for the dumper. *"Remember when you told me you'd love me forever?"* Romantic language is feeling based and usually expressed in the moment. Triggering old memories rarely works because as we know from the previous chapter, the dumper has already thought about all of that, and this only reminds them of how low their interest currently is in comparison to what it once was.

- ***Spinning in Circles:*** After everything has been said, the dumpee still can't accept the result, so they go through all the arguments again and again. The dumper then gets tired and cements in their position, upsetting the dumpee more because now they feel the dumper is getting cold. The more the dumper has to say the words out loud, the more they brainwash themselves into the position and grow emotionally tired, so they become less likely to ever change their mind.

- ***Name-calling:*** Breakups are painful, and when the dumpee feels hurt and abandoned, they may have some choice words for the dumper. This is a bad idea because it only re-enforces their decision to end the relationship because now neither of you can even communicate like adults anymore. If you're particularly talented at insulting people, you may also say something truly unforgettable which makes it harder for the dumper to ever forgive you.

- ***Making them feel Guilty:*** As kids, we often get what we want by throwing a tantrum. By acting like the victim of the situation, our parents or loved ones will come to our aid and stop our suffering. In breakups, the dumpee may try the same tactic. They will cry, beg, threaten to hurt themselves, whatever it takes to elicit sympathy from the dumper in the hopes that they will feel pity for how hurt they are and give them what they want. But the dumper already feels guilty and as an adult, being a helpless victim is less attractive. The more crushed you appear, the more guilty they feel, and the less likely they are to reconsider because they would not want to risk hurting you like this again.

- ***Disagree with all of their points:*** When we get defensive, we are just canceling the other person's offense, not really listening or communicating. If you don't want to break up, your bias will cause you to reject all of the dumper's points. This makes them feel unheard and as if they are right to leave because nothing would change if they stay, as their opinions aren't valid according to you.

How to be Broken Up With:

So now that we know what doesn't work, we have to take those lessons and figure out what does. What is the right way to be broken up with that will give you a clearer chance of reconciling in the future?

- **Listening:** Rather than countering their every move, listen to understand and not to respond. If they feel heard, then they will feel as if their feelings are valid and not something that simply generates conflict. If you can listen and understand what they think and why they think it, then you can ask them open questions like *'What do you think we could try differently?'* If they are the ones who feel as if they are coming up with solutions that would work for them, then it feels as if it may be able to be fixed because they are free to try, not ordered to stay. If they can't think of anything, you can make gentle recommendations, but if they shut them down, mirror them and back away.

- **Let them feel free:** Rather than telling them what they cannot do (leaving you), remind them that *this is okay and of course they don't have to do anything they don't want to do*. Remember that the dumper has been highly anxious in anticipation of this breakup, and by taking the pressure off, they feel more open and able to confide in you, as opposed to fearing how you may react which results in them hiding information to protect your feelings. Once they feel free, then they no longer feel as if you're trying to trap them. If they can choose to leave anytime, then they may realize that leaving isn't such a weighted decision that they can't reconsider mid-conversation or down the line.

- ***Agree and Re-frame:*** Rather than telling them they're wrong or justifying the times you have been unhappy, agree with them that certain aspects of your relationship are not working. Even laugh a little about it. But after agreeing, identify that *things have been very stressful for one or both of you lately, and it's no surprise it's taken a toll like this.* By gently re-framing this issue as stress-related, when they calm down or grieve later they have a simple explanation for what went wrong planted in their mind. The story of the breakup becomes "stress", which means it's an external temporary issue.

- ***Keep it short:*** After a few minutes, it's time to wrap it up. If any of you are repeating the same points, then there is nowhere to go but downhill.

- ***Put the ball gently in their court:*** Remind them that you don't agree with the decision and you still think there's more here, but that you understand, and if they reconsider or change their mind, to simply let you know. Then walk away and never look back. This way they're clear that this is their decision and that they can reach out when they're ready to.

CHAPTER 4

The Immediate Aftermath

Now that the traumatizing breakup conversation has occurred, both parties go their separate ways. The dumper is highly emotional and a little shocked at themselves. Their pent-up anxiety is released and they feel both excited and petrified of what they've just done. It sounds heartless, but they feel a certain level of pride because they were so scared of having the dreaded breakup conversation and now they have conquered their fear. They still care about the dumpee and wish they did not have to hurt them, but now that it's done, a weight has been lifted. And if the breakup conversation was particularly emotional, nasty or drawn out, they are relieved it's over. They did it and now it does not have to be repeated.

But oftentimes the dumpee has other plans. While the dumper feels like they just did a civic duty, the dumpee is often still coming to terms with the decision and is in total denial. The painful breakup conversation is a bit of a blur and they forget exactly what they did or did not say. The more minutes that tick by the more they experience separation anxiety. They worry they did not give a good account of themselves and their ***fight or flight instincts*** kick in. They re-write the past breakup as a conversation that spiraled out of control, not a serious decision contemplated and executed by their ex.

Now that they're in denial of what has just happened, they feel as if the relationship is actually only "slipping away" now every minute that they don't fight for it, because this isn't a real breakup unless they accept that it is. Remember that everyone justifies the decisions they make to themselves no matter how irrational. So in these panicked moments, they think of all those romantic movies they've watched where the protagonist makes a grand gesture or simply never takes 'no' for an answer, and they realize that this relationship isn't over, not until they quit, and winners never quit. So they pick up the phone and start texting or calling.

Due to the ***separation anxiety*** they are experiencing, their minds are haunting them with nothing but positive memories of the relationship they are now grieving. So they have become totally irrational, ignoring what was just said, in denial that anything was ever wrong in the relationship, and solely focused on recapturing the highlights of the past.

This is natural for any grieving process, but the excruciating difference between someone you love dying and someone you love breaking up with you, is that when someone breaks up with you, they're still alive, so they really could be spending time with you, but they're simply choosing not to. In reality, this is because they cared too much about you and your relationship did not work out, so it would only be painful for both of you to be around one another if a real relationship is no longer mutually desirable. But to the dumpee, it feels more like your ex has not died, but rather faked their own death just as a sly strategy to avoid spending time with you. This is why dumpees are often so offended when they spy on their ex's social media. It's as if they are thinking, *'You know I know you're not dead. I can see you. You're taking selfies so I know your phone works so you should be calling me if you cared about me!'*

This is not the case, but our egos are so damaged by the shock of the rejection that we lose sight of the fact that this person loved us and chose to spend a lot of their time with us. They shared intimate moments, conversations, and body parts with us. A euphoria was captured and shared, and a natural chemistry that no two other people have ever identically experienced is tattooed into the database of time itself, never to be undone. But rather than focus on appreciating what was, we become bitter about what could continue to be.

This is largely due to ***rejection***. When anyone rejects

us it makes us feel 'lesser than' and we wonder what may be wrong with us. On some level, modern society is built around certain qualifications and validations. Family shows you what it means to be loved, but school decides if you're smart enough to pass, employers decide if you're useful enough to pay, friends decide if you're fun enough to spend time with, social media decides if you're interesting enough to follow, and romantic partners decide if you're attractive enough to sleep with.

So when someone we consider a romantic partner, close friend, and possible future family member rejects us, it makes us feel that we may not be attractive, fun or lovable, thus jeopardizing our future plans to be happy, loved and married. This rejection breeds obsession. It's as if we now need that person back instantly to right the wrong, and to rebalance the chaos of the breakup. Why? Because we feel if someone could get so close to us and could then abandon us, that there must be something fundamentally wrong with us. And if there is something wrong with us then maybe everyone else we meet will identify the same thing and slowly but surely everyone we know and love will leave too.

We also feel a high degree of shame for how we felt, reacted or behaved during the breakup and want the other person to confirm that our behavior was "okay" because we now feel insecure that we are even likable, let alone lovable. It's as if all of our self-worth and future happiness lies in this person's hands. We compare our happiness with that person to the anxiety spiral without them and our mind attributes the vast difference in quality of life to our ex. Basically, our mind does a quick equation; *if life is great with them and shit without them, then they must be great and I must be shit.* So they now symbolize something far greater to us than they even really ever meant to us. They symbolize us proving there is nothing wrong with us to ourselves and to the world. All we need is their approval and validation. And if we cannot get them back, then we will forever feel as if we are on some level not unconditionally lovable.

So this sets the scene for two people who are on very different wavelengths. On some level, the dumper and dumpee have never been less compatible than this moment, as they currently have totally different needs. But the dumpee is trying to make them have the same needs again by dragging the dumper back into the breakup conversation. Dumpees subconsciously have a variety of different motivations when they begin to chase their ex in the immediate aftermath of a breakup; to convince the dumper to change their mind, to force the dumper to admit they still love them or to confirm that they really did love them at one time, to push the dumper to their emotional brink so that they can see they still care, to apologize and appease the dumper so that they can feel as if they are on the same page, or to stay in contact in any way possible so that they don't have to feel separation anxiety.

Unfortunately, when you've just been broken up with, your primal instincts at the time will push the one you want further away. If they don't want to hear from you, then you are smothering them and they will start to get colder and colder, typically re-reading from the same script as the breakup with less and less patience each time they have to explain themselves. If they are being kind to you and are willing to stay in contact, you will likely feel as if this is a great sign that is bringing you both closer together, but they see this as a way to close the book once and for all as they can't handle the pressure of your anxiety.

Dumpees often try a variety of submissive tactics to appease the dumper in case this quickly changes their mind. This can often include taking full responsibility for the failure of the relationship even if they did nothing majorly wrong. This is really just an attempt to cover all bases and "control the narrative". The dumpee feels so abandoned that they begin to agree with the dumper. It is as if they develop a weird sort of Stockholm Syndrome.

The dumper is typically surprised when they break up with their ex and then receive a series of understanding messages validating their decision and apologizing for wrongdoing. At this moment, the dumper's self-doubt is now reassured and it can motivate them more to push forward as you are telling them they deserve better, which feeds their ego. Think about it, if you just got mugged, you would not then message the mugger afterward, *"Hey, I just wanted to say, I'm really sorry for walking down your alleyway. I did not know it was your turf, but there is no excuse. You were right and I just hope there are no hard feelings.*" If you did not do anything significantly wrong, then you should not automatically be apologizing right away. This is why it's best to say nothing in the immediate aftermath of a breakup unless the dumper is contacting you first. You will likely always feel as if you have one more thing to say.

Other times, dumpees will be so ashamed of how they behaved during the breakup conversation or its immediate aftermath that they feel the need to send a **clean slate message**. These kinds of messages are a way of wiping away the memory of your bad behavior by signaling you are totally fine now and informing them that you are not going to chase anymore. But actions speak louder than words. If you are not going to chase them anymore then you do not need to message them to say that. That is submissive and on some level seeking approval. As if you want them to pat you on the head and say, "good dog". Nor do you have to apologize for how you reacted. *"Hey, I'm sorry I bled when you punched me in the face. It hurts less now and I hope your fist is not injured."* In extreme circumstances, a clean slate message may do no harm. You should not feel bad if you sent one. But generally speaking, it is unnecessary. It's usually done to make the dumpee feel better about how they have left things. But over time, if you stop chasing, then they will see that you learned your lesson and wonder more about why you chose to stop. They do not need you to punctuate your contact with a clean slate message that helps to give them closure.

In moments of desperation, dumpees may offer or accept friendship with their ex to soothe their anxiety. This makes the dumper feel like they've extended an olive branch and compromised. If they do follow through with being friends then disaster awaits. The dumper subconsciously uses the title of friendship to wean off the dumpee slowly, alleviating them of their own separation anxiety, and absolving them of any guilt they felt for breaking up in the first place.

Whereas the dumpee has now been demoted to ***"just friends"***, a role they have no real interest in playing. They instead see this as a clear stepping stone to being back together. Rather than come to terms with what has just happened or attempt to heal and gain perspective, the dumpee is now on a secret solo mission as an "undercover lover" in which they basically message, call or hang out together exactly the same amount as a romantic partner would (but minus any actual romance). They also see it as a strong strategic position to be in to scare away any new potential romantic threats to their ex. But knowing the dumper was willing to walk away cements an imbalance of interest, and the dumpee knows they are on thin ice. This makes the dumpee behave very subserviently to the ex that rejected them; they may start offering free rides, paying for things, or just acting incredibly nice to not risk pissing off the dumper any further. They do this in the hopes that the dumper will get so used to having them around that they are promoted back to romantic partner.

This is usually incredibly transparent to all friends and family of both the dumper and dumpee, but both parties will usually be in denial about it. If the dumper is confronted by friends and family, warning them to not "lead on" the dumpee, then they may feel guilty enough that they ask the dumpee to confirm that they accept that they are simply *"just friends"*. The dumpee will realize that if they don't agree, then they could be fully dumped, so they reassure the dumper that they accept their position. This creates severe unhappiness within the dumpee, leading to more insecure submissive behavior, but they tell themselves that this is better than nothing, and secretly expect that one day the dumper will be vulnerable or horny enough that things will just reignite between both of them.

More often than not though, the dumper will gradually distance themselves from their new foundfriend, the dumpee. They now have so many recent memories of them spending time with the dumpee just as friends, that they have mentally re-cast or re-categorized them as a plutonic character in their life with little to no sexual relevance. Realizing they run no risk of losing the dumpee as a person, they feel free to set their sights on new romantic partners, and when they find one, the new partner naturally sees straight through the dumpee's strategy and insists the dumper cut ties with them. This leaves the dumpee even more devastated, as they thought they were getting closer to their goal, but instead had a front-row seat to their own worst nightmare.

Accepting friendship with your ex is likely going to backfire and keep you in a state of denial, which drags out the pain of the breakup while helping them to get over you and move on. Be honest with yourself and your ex and don't accept friendship. You have too much chemistry for that and you would sooner disappear than lose your position as an exclusively romantic candidate in their mind.

So now that we know what is going on for both the dumper and dumpee, we have to carefully navigate around this emotional minefield. Mistakes around this period of time can be detrimental to your chances of reconciling in the short, medium or long term.

If you have just been broken up with and you feel you reacted badly, then stop making the same mistakes and cut contact with your ex. Change their name in your phone to 'Z', hide or mute their social media profiles so you do not see anything they post, save yourself from feeding your immediate obsessive impulses.

While you will feel you need reassurance from them that everything will be okay, identify that they are currently the least constructive person for you to talk to. Contact a close friend and tell them what happened. Spend time with those that love and care about you, and do not chase after your ex in any way. Remember that they have just made a critical decision and are unlikely to change their mind in the short-term, especially if you already disagreed with their decision a lot during the breakup conversation itself, to no avail.

The more you chase, beg, plead, or bombard them with messages or calls, the more "***awkward blood***" you will create between you both. "Awkward blood" is not bad blood per se, but it means that after some time passes, if your ex reconsiders getting back together or even just reaching out to you, they have a justified hesitation, because they remember how badly you reacted to the initial rejection, and they feel things may just be too awkward between you both. They also may fear hitting the hornet's nest because you may take this as a bigger sign that it is and resume the same chasing behavior as before.

Instead, walk away and never look back. Accept the decision. As much as it feels like you are letting them just slip away, you are likely only going to make the situation worse. And oddly, by walking away and not rewarding their behavior, they will gain more respect and attraction for you over time.

Why? Well, part of the reason that you crave this person so much is because they once loved you, but now they rejected you. So in your mind, suddenly this person becomes the best you could ever find.

It's as if all of our brains do a stupid equation: *If my Ex knows me and doesn't want me, then anyone who does want me must have lower standards than my Ex, and therefore have lower value than them. This means my Ex is the best I can do simply by virtue of not wanting me.*

If your ex no longer wanting you makes you feel like you need them more than ever, then we want your ex to feel that same way about you. They were anxious before breaking up with you because they anticipated that you would react badly. They likely had a whole set of worst-case scenarios playing through their mind. But if you don't chase after them, respectfully disagree and accept their decision, then you subvert their expectations.

Now they realize that they may have been overestimating their own value. And if they were so wrong about you and how they expected you would react, then what else were they wrong about? It undermines their decision. But if you confirm their expectations, or even surpass their worst nightmares, then they feel justified and like they made the right choice.

The dumper does not "like" it when the dumpee chases after them. It's an inconvenience and they hate hearing the cries of someone they care about. But on some level, it feeds their ego and reassures them that they are lovable and have a lot of value, because they are in the driving seat and turning down romantic opportunities, giving them an abundance mentality. Imagine someone called you right now and told you how much they loved you and would do anything to be with you, but you had to tell them that you're not interested. You'd feel pretty powerful, right? Don't give your ex that same comfort and satisfaction by validating their ego or their decision. You cannot reward negative behavior or you are subconsciously incentivizing more of it.

If they want to go, let them go. When they realize you are not chasing after them, they may feel a sense of relief at first because they had anticipated such a bad reaction. But that comfort does not last too long. Over time they start to wonder why they are not worthy of an overreaction, of a heartbroken call, or of any attempt to change their mind. *If you're not chasing me... Why not? What's wrong with me?* This sets them on the trajectory of feeling somewhat rejected back, which is exactly what you want them to feel to rebalance interest levels over time. Because as we know, rejection breeds obsession.

They will think more of you for not desperately wanting or needing them, and therefore any new romantic candidates that *do* feed their ego and want them, appear to have lower value simply by virtue of wanting them.

CHAPTER 5

Getting Yourself Back

The immediate aftermath of a breakup is total chaos and the dumpee may experience tremors of the emotional shock of the rejection for a long time. This is why it's important to start the healing process as soon as possible. In order to heal and to quite frankly stop making mistakes, dumpees should almost always implement a **No Contact** period permanently with their ex (there are a few exceptions we will discuss in a later chapter).

It's likely the last thing you want to do, so why is this the right move? Well firstly because at this point neither your presence within the relationship nor your objection to the breakup has caused the dumper to change their mind in any way. Therefore you should allow them to taste your absence. This way, you can stop making the same mistakes that will help the dumper cement in their position, while you surprise them with your strength and resolve, and begin the healing process. If the breakup becomes very messy and drawn out then the dumper can mentally never allow themselves to reconsider as they would not want to chance another breakup down the line. This is the painful and ironic part of chasing your ex after a breakup. All you want to do is make the most compelling argument possible to change their mind. But by doing so, you can push them so far away that even if they do miss you or reconsider what happened, they will not pursue it as they *"would not want to risk hurting you more"*.

Essentially, after a breakup has been imposed on you, you have a choice… you can enter No Contact right away. Or you can exhaust all possibilities, likely push your ex further away, and then concede that it's time for permanent no contact. Or worst-case scenario, never give up, get blocked or receive a restraining order. At a certain point, it is time to stop focusing on the person that has chosen to leave, and start focusing on the person left behind who isn't going anywhere… yourself.

No Contact is not a game, but a process. It is often used as a strategy to cause the dumper to change their mind. But from the thousands of cases I have dealt with, it certainly does not mean that you simply 'wait' for your ex to contact you, as many dumpees initially hope. It also does not mean that you stalk your ex's social media to figure out exactly where they are, who they're with, or what they're doing.

No Contact means that you do not initiate any physical contact with the person who has just rejected you. No texting, no calling, no gifts, no letters, no walking around their neighborhood for an "unexpected meeting"... but it also means no mental contact from your side either. So no 'liking' their social media posts, or even viewing their social media posts. Mute them, unfollow them, hide them, whatever it takes. You need to go cold turkey so that you can slowly but surely stop this anxiety spiral and deepening obsession about the person you have just lost.

This will initially sound impossible and goes against your every impulse because as mentioned in the previous chapter, most dumpees are in denial at first and feel that the relationship is only "slipping away" every minute they don't fight for it, rather than the decision already being made.

By sticking with no contact, your anxiety will subside over time. You will regain control over your emotions and your own destiny, which is vitally important. You will stop obsessively centering all of your behavior around getting your ex back and start to build a prosperous future for yourself. By taking care of you and constructing an active, happy life independently that you are proud of, you attract more people and opportunities to yourself... and that includes your ex.

But it's not easy. Most people I have worked with initially 'wait' for a few weeks, then slowly start to detach themselves, which they find scary. They often get tremors of the breakup and feel a sudden urge to contact the dumper in some way. This is why often times it helps to have certain mantras to say to yourself when you feel weak and like you should break no contact to start pursuing again.

Examples:

- Why would I do that? Why would I reward someone for walking out of my life and hurting me? That will only communicate to them that this is how I deserve to be treated and that they can do this again if they please. Because then I am beneath them. That is not right. I am worth more than that.

- Only they can change their own mind. Clearly my amazing debate skills did not convince them in the breakup already, so why would it help now?

- If I chase them, it will trigger the compassion part of their mind, not the attraction part. I refuse to let them take pity on me.

- Let's see what their intentions are. When I inflict their decision onto them. When they feel the consequence of their decision. I'll let them miss me.

- The relationship that I miss, those loving memories I cherish, I own at least half of that greatness... none of those memories could have happened without me.

- I don't even miss that other person, I miss myself. Who I was when I was back then. How happy I was. But I can be that again. And I will be that again.

- I'm scared because I fear losing them. But the worst has already happened. They're currently gone. And I'm still here, I'm still alive, I'm still me.

- If they want me gone forever, then I'm already at that worst-case scenario. This is that feeling already, that reality, and it cannot get any worse. It can only get better.

- This experience does not define me. This person does not define me. I define myself.

- I'm strong and attractive. If I got this person in the first place, then I can logically find someone just as good, if not better.

- This hurts me because I am facing the loss... so logically if I want them to experience the same sense of loss, I must not contact them.

- I'm going to surprise them, but I'm also going to surprise myself. I'm not chasing them. I'm accepting it. I'm moving on. If you want to stop me, then do the bare minimum and contact me yourself. Prove to me that you are worthy of my time.

- They determine their value to my life by whether or not they contact me… and if they don't, why would I possibly contact that person? Why would I inflate their ego and lower my own sense of self-worth?

- I've got a life to lead, not a life to give to someone else's whim. I control myself. I could change job, change country, change anything I want right now. I am beholden to no one but myself. This is liberating. I'm free.

- I have been in such close contact with this other person, part of me feels lost in them. But who am I? I'm more than I'm giving myself credit for right now.

- Now is my chance to get back in contact with my true self.

So now that you have the right mindset to help you to move forward, heal and get yourself back, it's important you start taking the right actions too. You take these actions for yourself, not because they will instantly make you feel good, but because you are planting seeds for personal growth that pay off in the future. You will not always want to do these activities, and you do not always have to, but sometimes it's important for your body to make the healthy decision in order for your mind to follow the same path.

Spend time with your friends and loved ones:

It's natural that when you go through a traumatizing loss that you will experience an anxiety spiral and depression. Maybe you're great at hiding your emotions, maybe you're not. But given we know that one of your biggest fears right now is that you are not unconditionally lovable, or maybe even likable, isolation will not help restore you back to your status quo. Letting your emotions out is necessary at times, but staying in and moping and crying is not beneficial to you. You should push yourself to remain active and not indulge in your worst impulses. What you focus on, grows. So let's not focus on the negative feelings. Instead, spend your time with those who love you and care about you while this rejection and loss processes in the background.

You can discuss the breakup with them, especially at first... but over time it is important to not consistently use your friends as a soundboard for all of your breakup thoughts and feelings. They will tolerate a certain amount, but after a while, they want to see some progress from you, which incentivizes them to keep doing more activities with you too. Also, it is not beneficial for your own progress to just talk about the breakup all the time, as what you focus on, grows. We do not want your ex or this loss to grow in importance in your mind. Joke around with your friends, and more importantly, ask them about the problems in their own lives. Hearing about other people's problems may initially make you feel as if they know nothing about suffering in comparison to your current agony. But the more you do it, the more you feel in touch with your humanity and realize you are a team together who care for one another. It's also a welcome distraction and trying to understand other people's problems can help to contextualize your own.

Exercise:

Sitting around and allowing yourself to get out of shape won't help anything. It's time to get that anxious energy out by exercising. Whether it be running, swimming, lifting weights, playing sports, boxing, whatever it takes. Getting blood pumping all around your body will lower your anxiety, and the results will give you more confidence in your body, which you should have. You might as well not just get your usual self back, but a leaner, more muscled version.

Go for walks in nature:
On top of exercise, it can also help to get away from the stresses of modern technology which may keep you in the same pattern of anxiety, instant gratification and stressful news and work updates. Whether you have a beach, a park, a forest or mountain nearby, check out the beautiful natural landscape to get you more in touch with yourself and your immediate surroundings. Watching the tide wash in and out, or listening to birds tweet, can be deeply therapeutic.

While music can help motivate you through intense exercise, it's not necessarily a great idea in the throes of a breakup, as music often dictates our emotions and when you're trying to re-center yourself, that's not going to be very helpful to you right now. Listening to love songs or inflicting a certain tempo on your mind can make it more difficult to find inner peace and clarity, as you are getting pulled back down emotional dead-ends that circulate the same words, emotions, and memories around your subconscious unnecessarily.

Focus back on hobbies you have always loved:
A lot of the time we lose sight of who we really are in a breakup and feel as if we are nothing without this other person. Sometimes that's because both of your lives have

become too intertwined, but in other cases, it's simply losing focus on the very thing that makes you, *you*. If you want to get yourself back, then it's time to get back in touch with your true passions and interests. Whether it be a certain sport, painting, reading, writing, gardening, photography, singing, stamp collecting, getting back in touch with something you love that belongs to you helps you to reconnect with who you were before you even met your partner. It reminds you of how much you have always had without them as well as what attracted, not only your ex, but others to you in the first place.

Work hard and level up in your career:

It's very easy to lose focus on your work-life when going through a personal crisis. However, work can be a welcome distraction that generates long-lasting rewards. Whether it be making more money, getting a promotion, networking or being a part of more projects, leveling up can get you back in touch with your competitive side in a healthy way. In the long run, you will be happier that you used this time to improve other areas of your life that were within your control, and can then reap the rewards for years to come.

Consider dating other people:

It's the last thing you want to do and rushing into a rebound is not recommended. But you do need to mentally stop thinking of your ex as your "one and only" and start thinking of them as "just another one". They are an option in your future, but not a priority anymore. Many people will refuse to date or flirt with moving on because they fear that the moment they do their relationship is officially over. Or that the dumper will find out and use this as a reason to start dating too. But that is willfully remaining in denial.

While you do need to take time to heal, opening your mind up to the idea of other romantic partners does not hinder your chances of reconciling with your ex in the future if they do return. They broke up with you, and accepting the reality that you are currently single is perfectly reasonable. Dating others can help you to get in touch with yourself again. You also start to remember what you bring to the table romantically and receive a much-needed reminder that you are attractive and have an abundance of options. Maintaining a scarcity mindset that your previous partner is the only person for you keeps you locked in a self-imposed mental prison for a lot longer than necessary. While you should never rush, when you do feel ready, you have no reason to resist.

Try new things and meet new people:
Often by repeating the same activities, you are re-treading the same water and recycling the same thought patterns.

But by trying new things and meeting new people you are pushing yourself out into the world and indulging in the present tense. When you indulge in the present tense you will realize that the future is an endless list of exciting possibilities that you are participating in.

For example, if you are always just around the same friends all the time, then on some level, you play the same role that they have come to expect of you. We often live up to other people's expectations of us, restricting our imaginations and desires, causing us to feel less free to explore. But if you start a new hobby that you go to alone, and meet a lot of new people with the same interest as you, you are on some level starting fresh and revealing your true self to them and now have a chance to make a strong first impression. This then reflects back to you and reconnects you with your own identity. Ask yourself: Who are you when you're alone? Who are you with someone new? Who are you with someone you've known for years? The more people you meet, the less concerned you become about what others think of you and that can make you more open to new experiences which will help you exponentially grow as a person in new directions.

Over time, this helps the past seem less relevant and the future seem more open-ended and exciting. And that will grant you a much clearer perspective of who you are, what you had in your last relationship and what your future could and should look like.

When struggling through a breakup it's important to remember that you are grieving. But as we discussed earlier, it's not quite the same as grieving someone that has died. So your emotions are battling internally between acting as if they are dead and gone, fighting for them to remain alive in your life, and confused as to what went wrong that lead to this loss in the first place. This jumbles up the grieving process to a new order. You may even cycle back and forth to different stages at different times when your anxiety spikes.

Denial:
When in the denial stage, you will say things to yourself along the lines of: *"This is not a real breakup, they will come back if I just convince them enough"*. This results in chasing the dumper even further away in a desperate attempt to undo their decision, because in your mind, the decision has not yet really been made, it is simply a mistake. So you are in denial. Then comes the spiral of sadness, but a refusal to try to feel better without the dumper returning: *"I will not start to heal or move on, because by doing so I am accepting the breakup decision and therefore making it real, which in turn makes them less likely to return, which they will, because this not a real breakup"*. This is very much akin to an emotional hunger strike, you protest the decision and refuse to get back to life until it's reversed.

Bargaining:

When in the bargaining stage, you have now realized that this is a real breakup and are willing to do or believe anything in order to counteract the decision. This often results in scouring the internet for answers and buying extortionately priced pamphlets of knowledge. At its best you may find useful material in your bargaining stage (hopefully this book), but at your worst, you may spend hundreds or thousands of dollars talking to someone on the phone for an hour, or throwing money at psychics, spellcasters and wizards who promise they have a super-secret serum that will bring your loved one back to you.

Anger:

When in the anger stage, you find yourself furious with the dumper for giving up on the relationship. Some days you vow to never take them back or even secretly plot to take them back and then dump them yourself just so they can feel this pain. This is usually the phase where you mentally dismiss your ex-lover as a "total bitch" or "complete asshole", viewing them as malicious. You may even begin to diagnose them with some sort of personality disorder in an attempt to understand how they could be so two-faced as to love you one day and then months or years later, not feel the same way anymore. Anger is a necessary stage to go through to not keep the dumper on a pedestal and realize what they did wrong in this relationship. It can help the dumpee identify that this relationship was not perfect which is a necessary step for healing and getting yourself back.

But sometimes people spiral down internet rabbit-holes in their anger phase which helps them to vent their frustrations about "men" or "women". Sadly this can have long-lasting negative implications like losing faith in meaningful romantic relationships or viewing sexual relationships as exclusively transactional as a way of protecting yourself from ever being hurt again.

Depression:
When in the depression stage, you don't want to go out or see anyone, you just want to cry alone in the dark. You may go to work or be around friends, but you just feel empty and detached from your emotions. You now realize the relationship is over and decide they will never come back, often viewing yourself as the problem and fearing that you may never find love again.

Acceptance:
When in the acceptance stage, you accept that the relationship is over and perhaps on some level needed to end due to its trajectory at the time. You are grateful for the experience, accept that you have learned lessons, and forgive yourself and your ex for your shortcomings. After all, we are all only human and they likely did the best they could to make the decision they thought was beneficial to everyone in the long run. You may still have hope for reconciliation, but you can accept any outcome and realize the ball is in their court now if they chose to leave.

You regain your confidence, maintain your social life

and get back to dating, aware that your past does not define you, and the future is unwritten, so all you can do is press forward with optimism that whatever comes next will be better than what preceded it.

CHAPTER 6

Take Your Ex Down from the Pedestal

In order to get yourself back and fully heal from this breakup, it's vitally important that you stop putting your ex on a pedestal as if they are the best thing to ever happen to you or the best you could ever do. They're not. And if you find yourself shaking your head and resisting that reality, you're probably using romanticized language like, "I'll never find anyone better than them". But that is just a story you are choosing to tell yourself, because right now, for whatever reason, you want that to be true. It's part of the denial stage in your grieving process. Because if you find better then you won't be as upset, and if you're not as upset, then you're accepting it, and if you accept it, then it's over… so your mind short circuits and says, 'Nope. Please no. I'll never find better than them.' Because what you're really saying is... 'I don't want to have to'. But you can, and if you choose to, you will.

Let's start this process by understanding it better. Rejection is the key reason that the dumpee will start to subconsciously **seek validation** from the dumper to ensure they do not get rejected again. Rejection toys with our minds. It makes us question if we are good enough for anyone, and for those that *do* want this post-rejection version of us, we often feel they are somewhat 'lesser than' for accepting us, because we know other "higher value" people have declined. A sort of, *'I wouldn't want to be a part of any club that would have me as a member,'* line of thinking. Being rejected makes us feel as if we're advertising secretly damaged goods to future romantic prospects.

After being rejected the dumpee often has a lot of doubts and insecurities about themselves. They want to ask the dumper to explain why they are abandoning them. They will rarely accept any answer unless it dramatically hurts their feelings because they feel as if there is a secret dark reason that the dumper is just being too polite to reveal.

Examples:

- What did I do wrong?

- Am I physically unattractive?

- Am I bad in bed?

- Why did you tell me you loved me back then if you don't now?

- Did you find someone better than me?

- Are you cheating on me already?

- Am I annoying?

- Did you hate spending time with me?

- Do you regret ever dating me?

- Is it that weird thing I do that only a few people know about?

- Is it my nose?

- Did I not communicate enough?

- Did I communicate too much?

- What is my least attractive quality— tell me, please tell me so I can fix it, good God just tell me!

Because you did not choose to end the relationship,

you feel as if you likely never could or would have, because according to all historical evidence, you never did. Therefore if you never left, the relationship must have been pretty perfect until it was stolen away from you for an unfair illusive reason like: 'loving you but not being *in love* with you.'

No matter how the relationship was going, and usually if you broke up, it had stopped going well for at least a few weeks or months or even years, we usually start to lie to ourselves. Rather than looking at the relationship objectively, and acknowledging what was not working, we rewrite the story of the breakup as entirely our fault. In our minds, we were the ones who were abandoned, so it must be all our fault, right?

But that's false, dumpees just tell themselves that story because on some level they are still bargaining with the world, and decide to subconsciously agree with the dumper that they are the problem. That way, if you promise to change in whatever way necessary, then the dumper will reverse their decision and fall back in love with you.

But what is near impossible for you to conceive of in the throes of rejection... is that there is likely nothing majorly wrong with you. This is because in your panicked anxious state, your mind compares your happiness with that person to the anxiety spiral without them, and attributes the vast difference in quality of life, to your ex. Basically, your mind automatically generates that equation; *if life is great with them and shit without them, then they must be great and I must be shit.*

So now they symbolize something greater to you than any one person has before. They symbolize you proving there is nothing fundamentally wrong with you. Perhaps it's insecurities from within the relationship, whether you're attractive or not, or how ashamed you are for how you reacted to the breakup. Whatever it is, you now start to seek the dumper's validation and construct all progress around the idea that if you improve enough or achieve something that they will return to validate that *now* you are good enough.

This can often set the dumpee on an unhealthy path where they find themselves mentally taking instructions for their ex-partner even though they're not there, which is like taking directions from a backseat driver who isn't even in the car anymore. So the dumpee is now sleepwalking through their present tense, miming the behaviors of a content and successful person building a future for themselves, but secretly only doing all of this with the motivation of getting back to the past and undoing the dumper's painful decision because it was so traumatizing for them. Only then will they be validated as truly lovable again.

Are you doing this right now? Ask yourself if you are secretly doing any of the following:

- Do I post on social media just in the hopes of getting a reaction from the dumper?

- Do I fantasize about succeeding in my career so the dumper will find out and regret their decision?

- Do I date or sleep around in the hopes the dumper will get jealous?

- Do I construct plans around times and locations I think I may "accidentally" run into the dumper?

- Do I travel to locations and do activities I know the dumper has always wanted to go to or do?

- Do I secretly hope the dumper is looking at my every move and therefore ensure they would be impressed with everything I do?

If so, you are on some level, living your life *for* someone else, and not being truly authentic.

But why is it that you can only think about the amazing times you had with your past partner? Simple, because you want this person back, and emotions influence the human memory. This is why eye-witness accounts of crimes are notoriously unreliable. When you have had a traumatizing or negative experience like being abandoned by someone you love, you rewrite the story of the breakup and the relationship to try to make sense of it all. The outcome of both of you breaking up becomes tangled with the motivation of you wanting them back. And this is why I say, the past is just a story you tell yourself.

An example would be, let's say you get into an argument with someone about a simple disagreement (their motivation being to debate or explain their opinion) and they say something that really hits a nerve with you (the outcome). Now what they said may actually be nothing objectively offensive, it just so happens that this issue is very personal to you. The story of that situation can become that this other person is totally insensitive and must have been aiming to hurt you (their motivation), because you are now hurt (your outcome). That way you can justify your reaction to what they said if in hindsight it looks a little over the top, because you assign a motivation to that person to justify your experienced emotional outcome. This is why everyone has a different account of events. All of our memories are filtered through our emotions, which are in constant fluctuation. So in other words, **your emotions influence your memory to create a false reality**.

Another way in which this can happen is that you want what you cannot have, and this bias clouds your judgment. An example would be that you are trying to book a venue for a party or a wedding, and it is no longer available. Now that the venue you wanted is unattainable, this means someone else booked it instead and stole your happiness. Your bias now influences your memory of the venue, causing you to put it up on a pedestal. Suddenly that venue becomes the best place ever and nowhere could ever compare, despite other venues being located more conveniently, costing less, or having better reviews. But because it's not your first choice, now it's merely a compromise.

These false realities we create in our minds don't last forever, as emotions pass. But habits form and we can short-circuit certain memories so they are stuck on a loop.

This translates to your breakup. The anxious emotion of wanting your romantic relationship back influences your memory. It causes you to numb all the negative times you had together to yourself. And this causes you to obsess and put your ex on a pedestal because you are telling yourself it was all perfect until you screwed it up. You probably notice that you always think of your relationship as your peak best romantic moments together, as opposed to your lowest moments together. The moments where you even secretly thought about ending things. But notice how swiftly you ignore that memory— dismissing it as not a real thought because you did not act on it, right? So your memory sort of skips from the amazing memory at the start of your romance, and then feels lost. As if perplexed how the dumper could throw that memory away, while actively ignoring the distance that grew between you; the uncertainty, the arguments, the feeling of giving up yourself.

The past is just a story you tell yourself. And your emotions about what you want to happen next alter that story so it will make sense to you and justify your current feeling.

As human beings, we need to justify our decisions to ourselves. We like all the pieces of the puzzle to fit together almost like a conspiracy theory. We cherry-pick certain memories, stories, and facts, to create a false reality that will motivate us towards our goal. A common example you will see all around you is in political discourse. People tend to be totally idealistic about what the ideology or policy they want implemented would be like. They have no idea if that would translate to reality of course. It often doesn't. But their goal is to have it implemented, so they will tell themselves the story that it would be incredible in order to motivate themselves and others to get the job done. Human beings are just wired that way. And a realistic political slogan saying, *"things will be a little better in this way but a little worse in that way,"* isn't very motivating for anyone.

And the same happens with your breakup. If you want a relationship back then you will not be able to tell yourself that the relationship itself was not perfect. You will make it *worth* wanting back in your imagination, to motivate yourself, by only playing the highlights. And this can be a dangerous fantasy to continue because no one can compete with that, not even the ex-lover you want back.

Because reality has ugly sides to it. And although you may acknowledge the facts that yes, they were pulling away, or we argued, or whatever, you don't allow yourself to feel what you felt at the time, which was likely anxious, uncertain, and even unhappy.

And that's okay. You can still want something that isn't perfect. But if you want something imperfect it's hard to obsess about it as much. And if your current goal is to get back together with your ex-lover, then it's best to not put them on a pedestal, so that you can heal and progress authentically. And when you are back in contact with them, that you won't get hugely anxious because this celebrity-like figure you've been dreaming about is actually talking to you. If you don't want to be disappointed by your ex when you talk to or see them again, then you cannot worship them. You must drag them into the muck with the rest of us.

But how can you do that? Where to even start? Well, it's not going to be an instant thing, but you have to start conditioning your mind slowly. I've constructed the following exercises in order to naturalize your ex as just another person, to focus on their flaws, to not idealize the past, to set terms and conditions for yourself if you should even reconsider taking them back, to mentally reverse the roles of dumper and dumpee, and to gain closure.

Exercise 1:
Normalize Your Ex

Your ex is just a person, but right now you're idolizing them like they're the President of your universe. Remember that many people who meet your ex are not very impressed with them. They see them as nothing special, just like how you likely meet a lot of your friends' romantic partners and think they're nothing particularly special. Even if they're gorgeous, you may secretly note that they're a bit self-centered or rude or immature or naive. They're nice or "fine" but they're not your type. The special version you experience with your ex is true, but so is the unimpressive version others see. Two things can be true at once.

But now it's time to view your ex from someone else's perspective. Think back to a time either a friend argued with your ex, or a stranger rolled their eyes at your ex, or a time they told you that someone they know dislikes them, a time that you factually know that someone really did not think much of your ex. And now, rather than defending your partner or dismissing that person's opinion like you would have done at the time... side with them.

Visualize their first impression or opinion of your ex from start-to-finish and what they must have thought about them. Just like you often find people inconvenient or irritating, others feel that way about your ex. They simply don't care.

Now you know it is possible to think that way. And the more you exercise that muscle of putting yourself in someone else's shoes and understanding why that person was right to not feel astonished by how simply amazing your ex is, you will recognize that you can too. All you have to do is simply choose to view your ex in any way you see fit. If the story you are telling yourself is not suiting you, then perhaps change the story by changing perspectives, and understanding that just like others are nothing special to you, your ex is nothing special to most people they meet.

Exercise 2:
Set Terms and Conditions For What You Want

While in the agonizing throes of a breakup, we often lose perspective about what we are even looking for in a potential partner. You cannot let go of the idea of your ex if you keep telling yourself that they are everything you have always been looking for. So let's gain some clarity and also set some terms and conditions for their return. Because it can't be as simple as them just clicking their fingers and they've won you over after everything they've put you through.

Write down a list of your ideal romantic partner's qualities from looks to personality to interests. Call it List One. Then on List Two write down your ex's biggest flaws. Don't hold back here, you know them very intimately.

You can name problems from within the relationship, how they dealt with the breakup, personal issues they have, anything, everything, write it all down. And now... compare the two lists. You want what's on list one, but here you are hoping that list two comes back. Crazy, huh? That is the rejection blinding you to your true desires. Unless your ex returns the right way, fixing at least some of the problems on list two, then you are seeking your Number One, because you deserve that, and there is no point in repeating the same mistakes in your next relationship. If you enter the same relationship with the same person and the same problems, you will likely just end up with the same outcome again.

The reason this is effective is that although your heart will initially deny that there is anything wrong, when you logically look at the two separate lists, your brain takes note of the fact that you may be making a mistake by telling yourself that you want someone with so many qualities that you don't actually desire. This forces you to think up ways in which they would need to change at least *something* for you to even accept them back, reversing the current power dynamic at play. If you think of them as if they are in the driving seat all the time, as if your fate and future happiness rests in their hands, then you are not being honest or realistic with yourself, and thinking submissively. But by starting to set terms and conditions, you are making a promise to yourself that the past actually was not good enough, and that no matter what, you will be entering a new healthier and even better relationship next, whether that be with your ex or someone else. This stops you from idealizing the past and look forward to the future.

Exercise 3:
Give Yourself Closure

Closure is often just an excuse we give ourselves to pursue what we want despite already knowing the outcome. A lot of the time the dumpee will insist that the dumper meets up with them one last time for "closure". These meetings usually devolve into a second breakup if the dumpee resists in any way, or else they leave things on good terms, which gives the dumper closure and resolves any unfinished business they may have felt about your relationship. It's best to leave behind unfinished business, as closure is essentially a confession of still being in denial. It's like telling someone, *"I need you to break up with me just one more time."* But closure can be beneficial in some ways. It can help you understand what went wrong in your relationship and resolve any uneasy inner conflict you have. So let's give you the comfort of having that closure, but not give your ex that same benefit.

On some level, there is a part of you that doesn't want them back, and you know there is. You can almost hear that whispering voice in the back of your head, but it's being drowned out by the dominating voice of rejection because now you can't have them. As we discussed earlier, this is because you're still seeking validation from this person and your mind is simply short-circuiting to the positive memories to justify still wanting them back.

Stop silencing that whispering voice. Listen to it. Focus on it. What's it saying to you?

Sometimes it helps to look back on those bad times with your ex. Those days when you were unhappy. Those days when you secretly thought of leaving, even if you did not fully mean it yet, even if it was just to spite them. Think of these moments as scenes in your life. Because they are. These are scenes from the story of your life.

But instead of that scene ending the way it did, write out the rest of that scene if things did not get better. Write it all out like it's a script for a play. Things get worse, the intimacy drops, the distance grows, that argument keeps going, whatever it may be... But no matter what, include you ending the scene by sitting them down and deciding that you do not want this relationship anymore. That you're sorry, but this just isn't worth it anymore. You have loved them, but you can't be with them. Then explain your legitimate reasons for why you don't see a future with them. Write that whole scene out.

And now, read over that scene. Understand that this is the reason you are no longer together... but this time it's you in control of your own destiny. You get it. There's no more searching for answers. You can see it as clear as day.

Then go outside or to your fireplace if you have one. And burn those pages. Watch it disappear into ash. It's gone now. It's over. You have just given yourself closure.

Exercise 4:
Let Go and Find Peace

While recovering from a breakup, both the dumper and dumpee will find themselves grieving the loss. But for the dumpee, it happens a lot earlier. They lie awake at night recycling over the same romantic highlights in the hopes that as long as they keep thinking about the relationship, then it's still alive somewhere in the Earth's atmosphere. As if you're emitting a cosmic energy as part of a Pagan ritual and you believe that as long as you keep performing that ritual then the dumper can somehow access that same thought from the universe.

This is all part of the grieving process. Our minds fear losing this person and do not want to allow it to happen, so they start to show us what we are losing. *"Look at it! Look how amazing it was! We can't lose this!"* And because you are feeling out of control, as you did not choose to end it yet, your mind is panicking and trying to hold onto anything it can... and all it can find is... memories. So now your mind is holding onto these memories like a clenched fist, refusing to let go. As if you're in an apocalyptic wasteland holding onto a photo of your loved in one hand, and a gun in the other hand, ready to fight off anyone that may try to steal your remaining possessions.

But no one can take away your history together. You will always be former lovers, you will always be two people who fell for one another and had an incredible time together. It is a fact. It happened. It cannot be undone. They're a part of you now. And you're a part of them. You may think you feel scarred from all of this. But no. These aren't scars. These are tattoos. They tell a story. The story of who you are and what you experienced. Be proud of them, not ashamed.

But just as that was who you both were together... that moment has passed, and like all of time, it's seamlessly blended into this present moment you're experiencing right now. Here. Look around the room you are in. This is now. This is you. This is all you have.

You can turn your neck around and look back at where you came from. Or you can keep looking forward. The way you're facing. The way you're going. The way that's revealing itself to you. Whether you think so or not, you are moving on, you are moving forward. Time is carrying you with it. There's no escape. So don't resist it. Join it. Embrace it.

That clenched fist in your mind. Picture it. Go further than that... clench your own first with your hand. Look at it right now. This fist represents you holding onto the past out of fear. Conquer that fear. Slowly open your palm, finger by finger. Every finger you release, imagine you can hear the stressed air burst out of it, like air out of a tire.

And now slowly open your hand up to an open palm. There it is. Calm. Relief. Phew. Whenever you notice your mind feeling overwhelmed and stressed, just tell yourself that your mind is like a clenched fist. And then picture your mind opening and closing like a hand. You're in control of it just like you're in control of your hand.

*Clenched fist…open palm… clenched fist…
open palm.*

Let go of it. Let it drift away. Stop holding on tight to what was, and focus on what is. You're here now, in this very room, and you're fine. You survived the relationship, the highs, the lows, the breakup, the pain, and now you're here. Ready for the next step.

By reading this chapter, you have just made the decision to move forward and stop hurting so much. You looked at this disgusting, treacherous swamp of a chapter and you decided that you would face your fear and push forward. Kudos to you. You could have not done that. You could have cowered away and gone back to calling your ex to tell them you miss them or stalking their social media. But you didn't. Acknowledge that you are already taking proactive healthy steps to get better… and therefore, are on the quickest road back home to the healthy mind you normally inhabit.

CHAPTER 7

The Stages of No Contact

Life is a strange journey filled with unexpected turns. You never know who is going to enter or exit your life at different junctures. Some may choose to leave, others will be forced to. As referenced in Chapter One, William Shakespeare's quote, 'All the world's a stage, and all the men and women merely players; They have their exits and their entrances; And one man in his time plays many parts.'[1] You never know who, when or how someone is going to re-enter your life. Often in the immediate aftermath of a breakup we find ourselves plotting someone else's return for them. Perhaps that's what makes you so uncomfortable about this situation.

Think of all your relationships, the people you have dated for short or long terms, people you loved and who loved you. These are all investments. And that's what the past is, it is an investment in your future. You invested time and feelings with these people. And now you move on to other opportunities while the past sits there in the background. Maybe it gathers interest, maybe it turns into a big pay-day. But you don't need to check on it. Rather, you need to go create more investment opportunities to create a successful and prosperous future for yourself. No contact is about taking a bad situation and transforming it into a series of potentially great outcomes.

Sometimes in a breakup, we can get lost in our separation anxiety and forget the fact that we too could have chosen to end the relationship. By putting yourself in the other person's position, answers regarding what to do can become a lot clearer. The dumper experiences feelings of *self-doubt, confusion, and guilt.*

If the dumper has doubts about their decision, why would you help them to feel they made the right choice by chasing them down and reminding them how attractive they are and how unattractive you fear you have become? The only feeling more powerful than desire itself is losing something great and fearing you can never get it back. It's the same fear that is likely driving you right now if you were the person left behind. So why would you alleviate the dumper of that same fear? Let them face the loss. Let them feel low-key rejected back. If they were confused about their decision and unsure what comes next then don't give them the comfort of your lust and adoration. Let them grieve and worry and wonder about you. If they felt hugely guilty about hurting you, then chasing after them or contacting them at any stage in a bid to win them back is likely just going to make them feel even more guilty for hurting you, as you are casting yourself as the "victim" of the situation, which is unattractive.

If you want to re-attract the dumper then you need to act based on their needs and divert their expectations, as opposed to satisfying your immediate anxious impulses.

Think of yourself as if you are in a business negotiation. The dumper has decided that they do not want a romantic relationship anymore, at least not right now. You, however, do want a romantic relationship. Why would either party change their mind? If you return to the negotiating table after being rejected trying to convince or concede, you are indicating that you have no other options. Therefore, you are in the weakest negotiating position possible. Why would they want to do business with you if they can see that you believe you could never find a better deal? That is desperate. By behaving this way, you are inflating their value in the negotiation and they realize that you need them far more than they need you. This helps them confirm that they made the right choice and that actually doing business with you would be a "losing" position.

In dating, most people do not like to think of themselves as "settling". They want someone equally attractive or even more attractive than they are. This is not all to do with looks but everything all encompassed; personality, sense of humor, future plans, finances, romantic chemistry, interests, and yes, fine, looks. If you act as if this person is the best you can do and behave that way, they will instinctively feel as if they deserve better than you as you are communicating that they are above you.

Whereas if you walk away and act as if you are strong enough to handle any outcome as you know you can find better, then their own self-doubt is more likely to kick in. At the very least, they will regain respect for you and stop thinking of you in a compassionate guilty tone. Rather than chasing them down, make yourself scarce and allow them to realize that you have other options and you do not need this deal as much as they do. The less available you are to them, the more they will assume you are doing great without them and could possibly be moving on with someone even better.

A famous 1991 study, 'Scarcity Effects on Value: A Quantitative Review of the Commodity Theory Literature'[2], concluded that people value something the less available it appears, as it signals to them that it is highly sought after.

When they start to realize that they actually do still have interest, then they have to re-evaluate their initial decision and slowly start conceding ground towards your side of the negotiation table through contact, meeting up and romance.

This way you are exploiting the weaknesses in their decision, as opposed to showcasing the strengths.

Part of the reason that no contact is an effective strategy is due to the **Fading Affect Bias**. What this means is that humans, of all genders and ages, tend to lose their negative emotional attachment to memories that have happened in their lives far more than positive memories. And over time, the fading affect bias actually just works more and more. The further away from the time of the incident, the less you will remember the negatives about it.

An example I like to use is, let's say you go on holiday to Vietnam for 10 days. You have an amazing 7 days, then you catch a stomach flu for the last 3 days of the trip and have a terrible flight home with a lot of turbulence. Now when you get home, your immediate reaction is, '*Ugh... what a bad flight. I am so glad to be back safe in my own bed, with my safe food and some peace and quiet.*'

But as more and more time passes, if friends or family ask, how was your trip to Vietnam? You'll say, '*Great! It's actually an amazing country, I had lots of fun,*' and you'll think of the fun positive experiences. The stomach flu is no longer a big deal even though it was 30% of the trip. You may even dismiss it as "not a big deal" or start realizing that it was partially your own fault for eating something very unusual from a street vendor. You'll make the story light-hearted and easy to digest for not only others, but for yourself, so you can forgive the past and not hold onto any stress or anger. The turbulent flight home is forgotten too. We remember highlights, not bad times.

And your ex will do the same with you. If the real meat of your relationship was good, then over time, that is what gets remembered. The sick times, the downward slump, that is not worth remembering. So it isn't. How can you be sure? Right now if I asked you to think back to a time you were sick, you could tell me the symptoms you had, but you can't *feel* what it felt like. That's why every flu you get feels like a fresh hell even though you've had very similar experiences before that you've chosen to forget. And this breakup (the turbulent ending to your journey together), whether you cried or begged or fought, over time that will get downplayed too. It will all be swept under the rug of the hysteria of the breakup.

We become more understanding with time. We take a step back from the impressionist painting that was our relationship and breakup, and start seeing something new that we never realized before. We gain perspective.

Most dumpees have initial doubts about going no contact with an ex. Their fight or flight instincts tell them that they must keep fighting for a relationship in order to get it back. They imagine that the dumper truly wants them to go away quietly so that they can simply move on. Therefore they vow to make as much noise as possible and make the dumper live to regret this with their constant advances or gestures of undying love. They do this in the hopes that they will eventually just concede and start dating them again out of pure convenience.

But dumpees tend to forget... your presence in the relationship and your active disagreement during the breakup was not enough to convince them to stay, so now you should let them taste your absence. If this person is worth fighting for this much, then allow them to prove themselves worthy of your love by simply doing the bare minimum, like contacting you. This is rarely what someone wants to hear in the throes of a breakup. They are more like to try to hunt down that perfect super-secret serum that some phony scientist has been developing in an underground lab or pay a spellcasting witch to change their ex's mind.

The fear of failure causes people to find excuses like, *"it will only work on men"*, or *"it will only work on women"*, because they have heard that it does not work 100% of the time. But of course, nothing can be that effective. The breakup has happened. We are in a tough spot right now. But I have seen literally thousands of breakup situations and can say that the majority of dumpers do reach out if you just leave them alone to face the loss. This does not always mean that full reconciliation occurs, but it puts you in the strongest negotiating position possible and causes the dumper to "break" first and re-open communication lines, which is a necessary step in rebalancing interest levels.

It also puts you in a stronger position in the long-term. Superdrug conducted a study called 'The One That Got Away'[3], and discovered that 71% of people still thought about former flames that they described as "the one that got away". 60% of which were fantasies about ex-boyfriend/girlfriends, and the rest were dispersed between former friends-with-benefits, ex-spouses, former flings, and even one-night stands. Human beings do reflect on great times they once had and idealize the past. This is why I put such emphasis on 'The Story of Your Breakup' because what is 'The One That Got Away'? It's a fantasy, an idealistic story people tell themselves, typically about an unresolved situation. Meaning there are lingering feelings of unfinished business. In the overwhelming majority of cases, no contact is the best way to make your story feel incomplete, and thus, make you appear more like the one that got away.

For men, it works because it doesn't play to their ego. If the woman does not chase him or reward his behavior and stops showing interest, he starts to wonder why his decision to leave has so little impact on her, while he is still upset from the breakup. His feeling of loss from the breakup will increase the less he feels she wants him. A

2000 study, 'Personality at Midlife: Stability, Intrinsic Maturation, and Response to Life Events'[4], concluded that men take a lot longer to process the failure of a significant relationship. So the less he is comforted with contact, the more time he has to fantasize about how great she must be doing in comparison to him. He will then suspect that she must be getting male attention elsewhere and is no longer interested in him. This rejection triggers his desire to hunt out of fear of losing her for good.

For women, it works because they need to respect the man to be attracted to him. When she realizes that he is not going to reward her behavior by chasing after her as she anticipated, she realizes how strong and stable he is, causing her to regain the respect for him that she may have lost in the breakup. She then begins to get curious about what he is doing in his life that keeps him so content without her. Women are more drawn to men who are active and independent. So breaking down and trying to win her over with cute cards, kind words and lovely gifts is unlikely to work. A 2010 study, 'He Loves Me, He Loves Me Not...'[5], concluded that women are more attracted to men whose feelings are unclear. So if the man makes himself look desperate and needy by consistently reciting his unreciprocated love for her, she loses respect and attraction for him. But if he is not chasing after her anymore, then it seems like he has an abundance of options, making him a high-value "catch" that is capable of finding better.

But as we discussed, no contact is not just a strategy to make the dumper miss you. It is also for you to heal, to lower your anxiety and to thrive independently. This way you can prove your worth not only to your ex but to yourself and the world. You must remember that you do not actually need your ex and will be totally fine without them. In my experience, successful no contact tends to unfold in five stages, the first three being the most important for the dumpee's healing process. Through each stage, the dumper and the dumpee need to gain and lose something. This causes them to change their state of mind, which, over time, rebalances the power within the relationship, which is necessary in order to be re-attracted to one another and reconcile.

The Five Stages of No Contact

1. Resisting

The Dumpee Gains:
Control of themselves back
After the initial shock of the breakup, the dumpee is resisting reality and searching for answers frantically on the internet. They refuse to accept the decision and start to write letters, text, call, whatever they need to do to get the dumper to hear them out just one last time. They also tend

to count the days, hours and minutes since they have last been in contact with their ex because every second feels like torture. They focus on constructing logical arguments in long-form for the dumper to read. This cycle can be addictive and although the dumpee is spinning in circles, they still feel they can't stop just "doing something" or else the relationship will be gone for good. This can cause the dumpee to lose their sense of self-respect and that in turn drags out their healing process for a lot longer due to the shame they feel for how they behaved.

But no contact gives them something to live by. They decide they've had enough and they are never going to chase the dumper again. If this person is worth their time anymore, they can do the bare minimum and reach out, otherwise, they vow to move on with their lives.

The Dumper Loses: Their Expectation

As wonderful a person as the dumpee thinks the dumper is, there is a small part of them that was enjoying the comfort of being chased by the person they rejected. It made them feel desirable, important and powerful. But then it either never happens or it just stops one day. And now that their expectations are not validated, they start to wonder about what else they may have been wrong about. So their expectations are undermined.

2. Rebuilding

The Dumpee Gains: An Understanding of Why the Breakup Happened

Time apart from the dumper gives the dumpee an understanding of what went wrong in the relationship. They start to realize the role they played in the breakup, as well as the role the dumper played. In this phase, the dumpee will stop panicking and start to gain perspective. They will take the dumper down the pedestal they were on in their mind and start rebuilding their self-esteem and their life (often from ground zero but it's a start).

The Dumpee Loses: Their Anxiety Spiral

In the resisting stage, the dumpee felt highly anxious, they could feel time ticking by in a state of panic. But now, their anxiety lowers and they find it easier to cope day-to-day. They may still count the days but it's less often and tends to be in larger units like weeks or months, as opposed to days and hours. They realize that they actually do not need their ex and can build a happy life without them, but still would like them back.

The Dumper Gains: Respect for the Dumpee

They feel relieved that the dumpee is no longer pressuring them to undo their decision, which makes them temporarily very pleased. They wonder about the dumpee from time to time and are glad to hear from others or through social media that they are doing well. They now respect the dumpee for not chasing after them and making both of their lives easier, as they recognize you both just went through a really tough experience together.

3. Resurfacing

The Dumpee Gains: Their Confidence Back

The anxiety of a breakup can often feel like drowning emotionally. But after some time, the dumpee resurfaces. Air bursts back into their lungs. They realize they are the authors of their own destiny and have a lust for life. They want to travel more, make new friends, spend more time with old friends and work on their career. This is the moment that the dumpee loses their tunnel vision on just doing all of this to win their ex back, and their life starts to feel more like an open road of endless opportunity. They remember who they were before the relationship and all the amazing qualities that they bring to the table. They grow so much they're not even sure if they would take their ex back, as they now realize they have so many other options.

The Dumpee Loses: Their Fear of the Future

The dumpee had a clear vision of what their future was going to look like... until the dumper shattered it in half. This caused the dumpee to feel deep uncertainty and pessimism about their future because their present was so unexpected and undesirable. It's as if they were lost on an island by themselves, petrified of what the future might hold. But then when their confidence returns, a bridge back to the future appears. They start looking forward instead of backward, and start living instead of waiting.

4. Reassessing

The Dumpee Gains: The Dumper's Attention

After weeks or months (or occasionally years), the dumper suddenly realizes that the dumpee is not going to contact them. They begin to feel foolish for ever expecting anything different. After all, they broke up with them. So they feel conflicted. But now that they are facing the loss they don't feel as comfortable about it at all. They feel a bit homesick because they are now far away from home. They start to stalk the dumpee on social media and are surprised to see how well they are doing (now that they are actively resurfacing).

The Dumper Loses: Their Sense of Security

The dumper once felt deeply secure with their decision, and on some level, expected this power dynamic to last forever. But now that they aren't being contacted whatsoever, they lose that sense of security in themselves. They debate contacting the dumpee but actually resist doing so for a while because they fear they may not even get a response.

They wonder if the dumpee is dating someone new or what is going on in their life that is clearly so much better than the relationship that they are now grieving. They initially felt relief, then they gained respect for the dumpee, but now they feel a little rejected back.

The Dumper Loses: Their Understanding of Why

They were initially very clear on their decision to end the relationship. But now that the Fading Affect Bias has taken place, and their own judgment is clouded by this feeling of losing control and being rejected back, they struggle to identify with their exact reasons for breaking up. Especially when they realize how well the dumpee is doing without them. The dumpee has had a totally different experience of coming to terms with what went wrong within the relationship in their rebuilding stage, but the dumper is only facing the loss now, and given that they were riddled with self-doubt and confusion at the time, they now question their decision more than ever.

5. Reconnection

The Dumper Loses: The Upper Hand

The tables turn and the dumper no longer feels guilty for hurting the dumpee, as the dumpee does not appear to be a victim in any way. They don't think of them in sympathetic terms like they used to. This helps the breakup feel a lot more mutual and balance has been restored. They swallow some of their pride and contact the dumpee in a nonchalant way to test the waters.

The Dumpee and Dumper Regain: A Romantic Relationship

After the dumper contacts the dumpee, they are both on a path towards reconnecting romantically. The dumpee learns a valuable lesson about their own value. They realize they did not need to panic because they will be totally fine with or without their partner. And the dumper learns a valuable lesson about the dumpee's value to their own life. Both parties now feel equal and satisfied that they are not settling but "leveling up", just like the first time they met, despite this being with their ex. This sets them on the healthiest path forward together.

CHAPTER 8

The Exceptions and Situations of No Contact

The Exceptions to No Contact

Although straight up no contact is the way to deal with 95% of breakups, there are of course exceptions in which no contact is either not possible, or is not immediately advisable due to the specifics of your situation.

If you ***took your ex for granted*** by not spending enough time with them, insulting them, cheating on them, whatever it may be, and the end result is that they feel neglected and as if you'll "never change"... then going directly into no contact is not going to prove their theory wrong. Instead, it may actually prove their point. But you need to careful here. This is a rare situation. Most people will try to think up minor infractions that qualify as taking their ex for granted so they can then use that to justify doing what they really want to do anyway (chasing after them). No. In order to know that your ex is breaking up with you because you took them for granted, they need to actually specify that they want to break up for that reason. That they are quitting because it has gotten so bad that they cannot see a future with you or have lost the desire to continue.

If that is the case, then you need to sit down and talk with them. If they are unwilling to meet to discuss this idea, then send them a message to talk on the phone or do it via text. Not too long-winded but express the following:

1. **Apologize.**

2. **Agree with them that you haven't been doing enough.**

3. **Identify what you did wrong.**

4. **Outline what is going to be different from now on.**

1. If you are to blame, you should take responsibility and apologize. But just saying the words isn't enough if this has been going on for some time. Anyone can say sorry even if they don't mean it.

2. That is why you then agree with them that you have not done enough—because if you get defensive, then you are deflecting blame and responsibility away from yourself, meaning nothing will change, therefore they are right to break up with you.

3. You then identify specific moments you were wrong and how. This isn't fully necessary if this communication is done via text, as you don't want it to be too long as that can look desperate and offputting. But by identifying specific moments and what you did wrong and should have done differently, your ex can see that you do understand. Anyone can say they are sorry, but if you say, *"Look, I agree with you, you're right, here are a couple times I know I should have done this and I'm disappointed I didn't. There is no excuse. I should have done better and I know I can in the future."* If you both agree with what's wrong, and you show insight into your own failings that they don't expect, then it sets you up in the clearest way possible for the final step of the exchange.

4. Outlining what will be different in the future. Then you propose what you will change. Maybe you'll quit a nasty habit, or cut down on a work schedule/ hobby that is causing you both to not have enough time together, or you'll listen more and be less defensive, or go on more trips and weekly dates. The point is you offer change and sacrifice.

You don't say this because you expect they will instantly change their mind, you do it because it's the right thing to do. If that is not enough for them, you go into No Contact and stay there. You give them the time and space to miss you and consider what you have said. Now the decision to break up is not based on you neglecting them. Now it is their refusal to allow you to try to fix the problem. This changes the story of the breakup in their mind which is important. Because this way, when they grieve and feel the loss, they have only themselves to blame. They cannot be angry at you because you did the right thing. You took responsibility, made no excuses, identified and empathized, even offered solutions. Any pain they feel now is out of their own stubbornness, not your neglect.

Others will not be able to implement no contact fully because they are still **_working with their ex_**. If you are both working together then you cannot simply just ignore one another. That will be unprofessional and could cause you to lose your job over time. Instead, simply treat your ex as if they are any other colleague. Discuss business matters with them exclusively. But do not seek them out. If there is a team project for two, you should not pick them just so you can use this as a chance to spend one-on-one time with them. The workplace is for work, not your personal issues. The break room is for breaks from work, not a place to tell your ex how much you've changed and want another shot. Outside of work, you remain in no contact and they must initiate with you.

An issue I have seen many times with my clients is that the office can become a bit of a battleground. If you go into no contact and hide away from them in the break room and isolate yourself, then you are handing over too much power to them. Over time, office politics can come into play, and people may start to "side" with your ex because they are all spending a lot more time together as you are hiding away in isolation. This can result in you feeling out of place and quitting your job, so ensure that you maintain your usual relationships at the office. If you go for lunch with a certain group, then keep going with them. If your ex is tagging along, just don't pay them much attention, but don't look hurt and decide not to go. That communicates to others that you are the victim of the breakup and they will get used to not having you around. It's your office too.

Be civil with your ex like any colleague or acquaintance. If they seek you out and start making peace and chatting now and then in the break room, then so be it. You can build these little interactions over time. But use work as an excuse to cut the exchanges short after the chat peaks and leave them wanting more. This way if they are showing a lot of interest, you can casually capitalize and ask them to get a drink or hang out outside of the office, because you have the excuse that you need to get back to work now. If you are already in the middle of a fun conversation then they are more likely to say 'yes'.

Another exception is if you are **living with your ex.** If neither of you move out after the breakup, then you are not going to be able to implement full no contact without driving the other person crazy or feeling as if you are immature. The silent treatment is just frustrating, not attractive, so don't go down that road. Simply implement minimal contact. That means that you go about your day and life as you normally would, and talk to them at the same rate you would any other roommate that you don't get on with incredibly well. No animosity, no arguments. Use this as a chance to remain active outside of the home so they can see that you are totally fine and continuing your life independently without them. This is a more attractive position than making their life difficult. If you demonstrate that you are active in society, tidy, considerate, easy to handle bills with, and easy to live with, then you do not fuel their decision to break up as you remind them that you still function well together.

Also, just because you live together, you should not turn the home into a 'breakup prison' that they can never leave, in which you constantly bring up the breakup at every opportunity or try to convince them to change their mind. Over time, they may warm to you bit by bit. If they do want to talk to you more and more over time, then slowly build up your interactions incrementally, so it feels like you are both slowly getting closer and closer to one another, almost like a magnetic current pulling you back together. Do not jump at the first point of contact and start smothering them. Let it build slowly, and if romance blossoms just enjoy it without pressure. Remember that pressure is the enemy of uncertainty and if they are luring themselves back in, you don't want to scare them off with immediate commitment negotiation.

Similarly, if you have **children with your ex**, then you cannot simply cut contact fully. Your kids are your priority and will not be sacrificed in order to try to prove a point to your ex. But outside of dealing with your children, whether it be arranging to collect them or drop them off, you don't remain in contact at all. They are only breaking no contact when they ask about *you*, not when they message or call exclusively to talk about the kids. In the meantime, you remain active and demonstrate what a good parent you are. By showcasing that you can still be civil and function well as a team, it undermines their decision to break up, as opposed to arguing, being bitter, late, or anything that fuels them to the conclusion that you just don't work together anymore.

The Situations of No Contact

Through answering thousands of emails, it's safe to say that breakups can be messy situations. As much as we may plan for everything to be clean and tidy, usually something will come out of left field that shocks you and disrupts your progress. The key is to never let your worst impulses take over and not revert back to the breakup conversation. If you do, it will make life awkward, they will feel frustrated and more often than not, they will just re-read from the same script as the breakup and get colder and colder every time they are forced into repeating themselves. So here are some common situations I have seen over the years.

Running into your Ex on the Street:

You're implementing no contact and feeling pretty great. Then one day you turn the corner and realize your ex is about to pass you on the street, or down a supermarket aisle. They're unavoidable. Your anxiety rises and you likely realize this is the worst you've ever looked and you literally wish this was happening at any other moment in your life than right now. What to do?

If they're on the other side of the street, just keep walking, you do not need to seek them out and start a conversation. That may not be what they want and by approaching them in an unnecessary situation, it confirms their suspicion that you are still chasing them in some way.

If you are passing them and it is unavoidable, then initially just grin, nod and stroll past with a muted 'hey' to see if they slow down or not. If they keep walking, then their anxiety is surpassing their manners and they are not ready to talk. Let them go. If they do slow down, have a brief warm exchange with them. Don't launch into a story about how amazing your life is now, especially if they did not ask. This will come across as you seeking their validation, lying, or boasting. None of which is a good look. Simply seem at peace. You want their impression to be that you seem well, active and content. A different image than they had the last time you spoke, which was likely when you seemed upset during the breakup. So no matter what, do not slip back into trying to change their mind. It's predictable and only feeds their ego. A quick conversation— pleasant, warm, at peace, then you're going along on your merry way.

Running into your Ex at a Party:

Weeks or months after the breakup, you are invited to a party that you highly suspect or even know your ex is going to. You will naturally want to avoid this social event. But if the host is a close friend of yours, then you should value that and go.

If you have not befriended them for a long time after the split and have been in no contact, then your ex will likely still have emotions tethered to you and what happened. There is this big mystery for them about what you're like now, whether you are still angry or upset, and low key, if you are still interested or not. This is why it's vitally important that no matter what, you do not use this as an opportunity to try to win them back into a committed relationship. That will only indicate to them that you are still living in the past, and in the environment of a party, it will only highlight that you are obsessed and have done nothing with yourself since the breakup except wait for a chance to see them in person so you can go back to begging and pleading. It's a low-value move that will only serve to inflate their ego.

But some people wonder if it is breaking no contact to engage your ex in conversation at the party? The short answer is... No. It's not. As long as you feel ready and it isn't too close to the breakup or trauma then you should not be avoiding social situations, unless they really don't appeal to you. It's not breaking No Contact. It's actually both of you meeting on neutral ground.

Remember, it's a party. It's a place to have fun and socialize. If your ex is right there in front of you, inches away from your face, and you say nothing, then it does not look strong. It looks weak and rather childish. It turns into the silent treatment. So do not do that.

Instead, divide your attention and affection on lots of people in the room, male and female. When you engage with your ex, have a fun, light and brief exchange, talking in the present and future tense, no mention of the past or the breakup. Then when your short chat peaks (meaning maybe you crack a joke and your ex or their group of friends are amused), you walk off like a social butterfly as you are too fun, confident and social to stick around. Why do this?

Firstly, it's not awkward. And that actually goes a long way because part of them was worried this whole party was going to be underpinned with awkwardness.

Secondly, it shows that they are not a key priority for you. They likely figured when you started talking to them that this could turn into you never leaving their side and them just letting you down easy or having to avoid you, but instead you steal their thunder by walking off.

Thirdly, it causes them to wonder about you while you are gone. Attraction can grow in that space. Think about it, what's better? Someone who sticks around for too long or not long enough? Leave them wanting more. They will likely find themselves secretly watching you talk with other people, especially people they consider potential romantic match-ups for you. While they are wondering this, you are now in their head as an attractive candidate for the world. Good! Because you are one. Once they think of you as someone attractive and capable, it reminds them why they were with you in the first place, and why others will too. This is a totally different vibe than if you were obsessively never leaving their side, or talking about the breakup, or avoiding them awkwardly. One is attractive and commanding, a social magnetic force that draws attention. The other is a charity case and a burden to be dealt with or tolerated, not enjoyed.

As the night progresses and you feel social, then you can develop these small chats with your ex to medium length chats if it's going well. If people are drinking and having fun, they will likely want to talk to you just one-on-one.

Treat them like anyone else other new person at the party or social event that you might be flirting with. Fun moments in public that can lead to situations alone in private.

If you're not used to doing this, use inside jokes or develop little improvisational dynamics throughout the evening so that you bounce off each other well. Inside jokes and even improv are useful because it creates a little world that only you both inhabit.

Rebounds:

As tough as it is to accept, after a breakup, both people are now single. A lot of dumpees will remain in denial about this fact and consider themselves still in the relationship until the dumper physically dates or hooks up with someone else. This is a bad strategy for personal healing, as firstly it relies on remaining in denial and not accepting reality. But secondly, because it allows the dumpee to feel betrayed whenever their ex finally engages in romantic or sexual activity with someone else, despite them being single. This can leave behind a false feeling of being cheated on for the dumpee. That emotional baggage can then be carried into future relationships despite the trust *in* that relationship not actually being broken, except for the decision to end the relationship itself.

A lot of the time, the dumper or the dumpee will fall into a rebound relationship after the breakup. Rebound relationships should not be mistaken for monkey branches, which means that the dumper lines up someone new, then starts detaching from their current partner while attaching to their new partner. They then break up with their current partner and swing across to their new partner.

Whereas a rebound is when someone is still in the process of recovering from a breakup so aren't really ready for a new relationship. But in order to help themselves get through the pain of the separation, they start dating and sometimes jump into another seemingly very serious relationship very quickly.

The most obvious symptoms of a rebound relationship are:

- They are just out of a relationship with a person they had very strong feelings for (within 2 months usually, it could be longer, sometimes it's just the next person they date no matter how long, but usually it means the pain of the loss is still fresh).

- They graduate to advanced levels of a relationship

fast because internally they don't want to feel like they have really lost anything. So for example, if they were living with their ex, they may suddenly jump into living with this new person very early on in their new relationship because that way they don't feel as if they are downgrading. They were in a level 8 relationship and now they still are. Nice and tidy.

- They talk about their ex a lot. They may even still be in communication with them.

- Or they are recently out of a breakup yet never mention their ex whatsoever. As if they are intentionally just dodging those memories as it is too painful. These are symptoms that someone is processing a loss and usually means that they are not emotionally available long-term.

While in a rebound relationship, the person who is rebounding will not know they are rebounding because they are somewhat in denial. Instead, they find themselves feeling an abnormal level of comfort in someone they have just met. This is because they are projecting all of that love, energy and future expectations from the previous relationship onto this new one. The problem with rebounds is that they appear very genuine. This causes the single ex who is not rebounding a lot of pain and confusion.

But from what I've seen, unlike monkey branch situations, rebounds tend not to last. This is because the person rebounding is in a somewhat altered state. Although the feelings feel very real, they are more of a snapshot in time than the full picture. The best dating comparison I can make is a *vacation fling*. If you go on vacation to a paradise island for two weeks of relaxation, you may meet someone and start a romantic fling. As fun and powerful as that romantic fling feels in the bubble of your vacation, it rarely ever translates to the real world if you were to both try to really date when you get home, or if you were to move to one another's city. It's a whole different reality, a different setting, a different universe. There's work, social obligations, being tired, stressed, sick, or just bad weather. There's a full other life to adapt to and this one moment, in this one location and one version of this person that you experienced in your two weeks together, often doesn't translate to long-term compatibility.

And a rebound is kind of the same; they look the same, have the same voice, the same sense of humor, they say the same romantic things, and they make big plans and gestures... but they're not home. They're internally abroad. And if they are disguising their grieving with a new relationship, it's like they're away on vacation. Yes, they're having fun, but with all the stresses and difficulties of their life still at home waiting for them.

But if the dumper is rebounding, it's a very painful and confusing feeling for the dumpee to watch them jump into another serious relationship so soon. It naturally sparks jealousy and they even begin to wonder if perhaps this was all going on behind their back because it seems so advanced, happy and real. The worst thing a dumpee can do is confront their ex about their new rebound. Acting jealous or crazy will typically just push the dumper further into their rebound's arms.

Why? Because when you act jealous, you are communicating that you see the value that this other person brings to the table. That you are intimidated by how much better they are than you. This actually validates the dumper's decision to be with this other person. It also lowers your value as you look angry, crazy and bitter. The new person then comes across as very strong and stable simply by virtue of not overreacting or caring. So you automatically stack the deck against yourself, giving the new rebound guy/girl far more ways to win and yourself far more ways to lose.

Additionally, by creating conflict, you are inadvertently creating an "in" and "out" group. You cast yourself as the leader of the "out" group while pairing the new couple inside the "in" group together. They can now bond more in that group because they have a common enemy (you) and any drama you create only fuels their romance more, because you are making it on some level, forbidden, and therefore taboo. No one likes to be coerced or told what they can't do, so by instructing your ex to obey you, despite you no longer being together, they are more likely to rebel against you, and will now even hook-up with or rebound with this new person as a way of demonstrating to themselves that they are no longer under your control because your relationship is over.

So unfortunately, if you want your ex's rebound relationship to end, your best strategy is to just let it run its course in its own time. Your interference will likely just backfire.

CHAPTER 9

Social Media and Breakups

Social media has become deeply ingrained in our day-to-day lives. Most people will come to the logical conclusion that social media is bad for them, but will be unable to stop themselves using it out of fear of becoming disconnected from their friends and the world at large. We all know that one principled person who was so morally against social media that they refused to make an account or participate. We admired their courage. But they subsequently missed out on so many social gatherings over the years that you just never saw them again.

Social media is a strange landscape that encompasses most of humanity's rawest desires. The opportunity to be seen and heard by anyone and everyone presents a sort of equal opportunities platform. And in the pursuit of followers, there is no limit to how low someone may go. They'll donate their most intimate thoughts, their nude photographs, their mental health problems... whatever it takes. Social media takes the principle of a celebrity magazine; the gossip, the high-profile party pictures, and says, '*Here, you go create your own*'. Choose the lives you deem worthy of reading about. Read about the people you know and the people you wish you knew.

In many respects, the paparazzi have become obsolete, we've been tricked into doing their job for them now that every smartphone has a camera lens on its front and back. And with one click, it's published forever, a photograph of you with your head wrapped around an unflushed toilet. Or worse, you're filming yourself. Walk into any nightclub and you'll witness everyone alone performing for their followers like some sort of undercover reporter. When we all get old and die it's going to feel as if we're being kicked off some sort of reality TV show. Your whole life will be flashing before your eyes in the form of a 'best bits' slideshow of your self-documented life. Remember that group photo? No? Maybe you would have if you hadn't taken twelve million of them.

It's as if we live under some terrible fascist regime where we have to do everything once for us and once for social media. Everything feels like some sort of PR stunt; birthdays, holidays, filming a full concert on your phone in one-minute segments to prove you were there. We've all seen it. Get almost any group of young girls together and it inevitably turns into a photo shoot. Because we're all in competition to give the impression that our lives are the best, that our lives are enviable, and of course, that our lives are worthy of publication.

And then your breakup happens.

Let's start with the basics. ***Should you delete your ex on social media?*** No, not officially. We don't want to send any signals that make you look overly distraught or bitter about the decision. Over time, we want things to neutralize and feel balanced between you both again. This will be established via zero chasing or validation ever being done on your behalf. But remember that you are in No Contact on social media too, which means, of course you do not physically contact them. But it also means that by seeing their face you are on some level still psychologically in one-way contact with them, so you should <u>not</u> look at their social media. This means that although you can remain "Friends" or still be "Following" one another for appearance sakes, you should hide, mute or unfollow their profile. You must not allow yourself to give in and feed this addiction of thinking about your ex.

The reason being that by looking at their social media you will begin to obsess about every little thing they do or post or like. Through the thousands of emails

I have answered, there is a clear trend that people struggling through a breakup read too much into their ex's social media activity. *Why did they post this song? Are they trying to communicate with me? Who is this new friend they added? I saw they were at a restaurant we used to go to— are they trying to make me jealous?*

By looking at their social media you are keeping your ex as an active cast member of your imagination and it will delay your healing progress. A 2010 study, 'Reward, Addiction, and Emotion Regulation Systems Associated With Rejection in Love'[6], from the Journal of Neurophysiology confirmed that "addiction" characteristics were present throughout a breakup. The researchers took MRI scans of people who were going through a breakup while showing them photos of their ex. The results showed clear neural activity associated with craving and addiction. So we want your ex to fall into this trap and eventually secretly spy on your social media, while you fully heal and always avoid theirs.

This addiction problem is often why the dumper may unfollow, unfriend or even block the dumpee. This usually causes an anxiety spiral for the dumpee as it feels as if they are getting broken up with all over again. This is usually the clearest indication of someone who was too invested in the dumper's social media activity. This is why I do not recommend looking at their social media posts whatsoever. If you invest in the idea that they are watching your Instagram stories or still technically following you, then you will be devastated if they stop doing it one day, or it may launch you into erratic behavior online in order to recapture their attention.

Being **blocked** is naturally one of the most painful experiences for the dumpee. If the dumper is blocked they will also take an emotional hit, but they will at least understand why it is happening as they chose to break up with the dumpee and may feel the dumpee is moving on or enacting revenge. Whereas for the dumpee, being blocked weeks or months after the breakup usually feels as if the dumper is intentionally trying to hurt them or hiding the fact that they are now publicly dating someone else.

So what to do if you are blocked? Nothing. Most exes block you from their social media in order to heal and move on. Perhaps they found themselves obsessing about your social media activity, or else they never felt free posting anything out of awareness that you may be observing them. They also may just be feeling angry or sad one day and have made an impulsive decision. Or else they are testing to see if you would notice if they blocked you as they have an eerie feeling that you are stalking their social media every day. If you overreact to being blocked and contact your ex to confront them about it, then you are basically proving that they were right to block you in the first place, as you were watching their every move. If you fight with them about being blocked, the situation grows more toxic and you run the risk of them taking it a step further (legal action). You should not even notice that they blocked you because you should not be looking at their social media in any way.

The reason being blocked hurts the dumpee so much is that they feel the dumper is making a declaration to the world that their relationship meant *nothing* and can simply be dumped and forgotten about. Being blocked feels as if they despise you and they regret ever dating you so much that they do not wish to ever remember that you even existed. These are the dumpee's biggest fears, not only being abandoned but forgotten, and are usually mirror images of how the dumpee felt in the immediate aftermath of a breakup.

But being blocked is not a sign that you meant nothing to your ex. On the contrary, you meant too much to them. You have to remember that unlike you, after a breakup they aim to let go and move on. They are living in the story that they chose to break up with you and are now moving forward. So if they find themselves grieving the loss of the relationship, as they naturally will, they may decide that they need to block you because the pain is too much for them. Knowing that you shared such a euphoric love high with them that they thought would last forever is agonizing to them because it did not work out. Seeing your name and face now serves as a reminder to them that they have failed someone, that love does not always work out, and it lowers their confidence in their own judgment moving forward. So they have to cut you out of their life because you meant too much to them. They can't handle the reminders of what once was because they currently do not believe it will be again.

Blocking is usually a temporary phase of a breakup. While it can happen that the dumper has started seeing someone else and doesn't want you to know, it is more likely that they are using this is a chance to heal. When they feel a little stronger or fear that this selfish decision may have sent the "wrong signal" they will likely unblock you one day. If you notice you are unblocked, this is not an open invitation to contact. If you do immediately contact them, then it will again show you are obsessively watching their every move and it will push them further away. You should not notice being blocked or unblocked, because, you guessed it, you should not be looking at their social media in the first place.

But **what should I NOT post on my social media after a breakup?** Naturally, after a breakup, you will examine your social media activity closer than ever because you realize it is a window into your life and you now want to harness this power to secretly communicate with your ex via your profile. It's the perfect plan. Make your life seem so good that your ex has no other choice but to return to you. Stop.

This is likely not a great idea and can easily backfire. If you rarely ever use social media, now is not the time to start posting every single day. That will look abnormal. The key to your social media activity after a breakup is that it should be somewhat similar to your behavior beforehand. We want you to appear unphased by the breakup, not desperately seeking validation, or worse, their specific attention.

If you are someone who maintains regular or occasional posting on social media, then you can maintain that. Although if you post daily then it may be time to reduce your social media activity for your own mental health. Whether you like to believe so or not, you will be subconsciously evaluating how each and every update and post you make may be interpreted by the person whose loss you are currently grieving.

Do not post pictures to intentionally make your ex jealous. If you decide to start dating again, that's fine. But posting publicly about it is likely not something you would have normally considered unless the relationship has progressed and is going somewhere. Posting a picture of you kissing your first date on the cheek with a caption about how you've never known love like this before, will either be interpreted as a pathetically transparent attempt at making them jealous, or definitive evidence that you are publicly rebounding.

Do not post depressing status updates, song lyrics or captions. It's great that you have emotions and you want to let them out. But perhaps this is the time to start privately journaling how you are feeling as opposed to posting publicly about it. Going to a counselor to talk things through is a lot more helpful than posting sad song lyrics. Remember, you do not want to appear like the victim of the breakup because that makes it harder for them to reconsider you as a possible candidate again in the future. It's normal to be sad, but taking the extra step of posting it on social media signals that you are deeply hurt.

Do not try to cryptically communicate with your ex via your social media. Sometimes when struggling to maintain No Contact, you may decide that you are too impatient to wait around for your ex to reach out. So you devise a totally subtle and not at all obvious plan like posting something that only they know about on your social media. Maybe it's an inside joke, or a scene from a movie they love, or a place you used to go together, or an old photo with a caption stating you have a lot of great memories there. Heartwarming stuff. But this will be very transparent. If your ex feels you are trying to either manipulate them or that your social media has become difficult for them to look at, they are more likely to disconnect or block you.

Okay, so those are the key things to avoid. But then ***what should you post on your social media?***

Accomplishments. As long as you are subtle about it, posting about positive things that have happened in your life is normal and can also be admirable. It's not a time to brag, no one likes a bragger. But posting that you have achieved certain long-term goals that you had throughout your relationship is a clear indication that your life is still moving forward. Your ex is more likely to regret not being there for this milestone or major achievement if it's something you have personally been working towards for a long time. This is more appealing if it's something integral to your life or personality like graduating, a career-achievement, landing a great job, moving into your new home, etc.

Travel. According to social media posts, all anyone ever does these days is travel. We tend to document our arrival at a travel destination as if we have discovered uncharted lands. We then post photos of ourselves in front of generic coastal backgrounds like we are Neil Armstrong taking his first steps on the moon. Not really of course, but let's just say posting travel pictures is a social norm. It showcases your adventurous, culturally enriched, fun side. If your relationship became boring and complacent, seeing you outside the house, trying new things in exotic locations with perfect lighting is always something that causes a tinge of envy in anyone who sees it. But with an ex-lover, they will view those photos with a heightened awareness that they could have literally been there with you experiencing all of this, causing a subtle regret and potential future FOMO (Fear of Missing Out).

Social activities. Being active is attractive. You don't need to post every single thing you do, but seeing you at social events or engaging in interest and hobbies is the best way to showcase who you are and what your life is all about. Being around others provides social proof that a lot of people enjoy spending time with you, and after a breakup, your ex will be curious if you have broken down or if you are still out there enjoying your life (which you should be).

But overall your social media activity should be less frequent. Do not post every little thing that happens to you. Only occasional highlights. Remember that human beings value things that are *scarce*. When something is abundant, then its value lowers. If you only post scarcely, then getting a glimpse of you becomes something rare that needs to be paid attention to and appreciated. This means that everything that happens in between these clear highlights is a total mystery and spikes their curiosity. Not being able to track each step between highlights makes your ex realize they are out of the loop, and being broken up means they will keep missing out on those behind-the-scenes details.

The best approach is not to center your social media around your ex at all. Remember they are currently choosing not to be a part of your life, so do not reward them by considering them in your present and future. Rather, use your social media to reflect your own life (if you choose to use it at all) and as an assistant to attract new partners. Remember that your thoughts dictate your feelings and your feelings direct your behavior. This is why people give tells in poker. If you are subconsciously targeting all your social media activity towards your ex, in the hopes that even if they're not looking now that they might one day, then that will bleed through to your behavior and on some level, your ex may sense that you are tailoring your decisions around them. But if your aim is to be happy and you seem more focused on attracting a new abundance of options, then your social media develops a life of its own, and any attention it gathers from others provides social proof to your ex that you are valued and more authentic.

What if your ex starts liking a lot of your social media posts? Well, sometimes exes maintain liking your posts in order to ensure that you are both still on friendly terms as they feel somewhat guilty for breaking up. So if they have never stopped, then this likely does not mean anything. It is not a reason to break no contact at all.

If your ex has taken a long gap away from liking your social media posts, or unfollowed/blocked you then re-follows or restarts liking a few posts, then this is a warm signal, but still does not warrant you reaching out to them.

Keep in mind, they may just be testing the waters, and if you overreact to such a small gesture, then it gives them the impression that you are still waiting on the sidelines for them. Just like how you don't contact each and every friend that likes a post of yours on social media, you don't need to contact your ex because they clicked a little button.

But I know that it feels different when it comes to romantic relationships. When anyone we have been romantic with likes a post of ours, it feels as if they are intentionally giving us a little ego boost or letting us know there is still *something there*. That an unspoken conversation about mutual attraction is taking place. This is why couples regularly argue if either partner remains in contact with their ex or dares to like a single social media post of theirs.

If you have a highly avoidant ex that disappeared from your life for a long time, then returns to your social media months later, liking your posts, then this may be them looking for a safe excuse to contact. A green light of sorts. This can happen with cautious avoidant types. They're not really sure what they're doing, but on some level, they are slowly luring themselves back in and just need to feel as if the other person made a gesture. I've seen this work many times, where they like 3 or 4 of your posts, and you simply throw them a bone and like one of theirs back (their next one, not an old one). Then before you know it they are back in contact making small talk. Just ensure that no matter what, you are always giving them less than they are giving you, you should not match or exceed their interest level if they are the ones that broke up with you.

This may all sound nice, but ***do exes even look at one another's social media?*** It's a natural fear to have. Maybe they have blocked, unfriended, unfollowed, muted or hidden your profile. But that does not mean they cannot easily find a way to secretly look at it. Most social media accounts are accessible publicly anyway. But failing that, a survey from 2018 by Tech.Co confirmed that 26% of people were happy to create fake profiles in order to comfortably keep tabs on their ex-partners.[7]

But of course, there is no way of guaranteeing that they will look at your social media. This is why you post for yourself, not them. But, there was a study undertaken by Superdrug which discovered that 56.5% of single Americans admitted to still looking at their ex's social media.[8] You may think that's nice, but once your ex dates someone else, then they will stop, right? Well, no actually. The number rises to 65.8% of married Americans, and then yet again, rises even higher to 66.7% of people in a relationship.

This is why I recommend maintaining No Contact permanently and not just for a limited amount of time. The types of relationships that exes will reflect on and wonder about for possible years to come are likely those that still feel on some level… incomplete. And if you can maintain your dignity, and don't provide full closure by having constant contact or leaving behind any animosity, then curiosity is likely to build over time, especially with the Fading Affect Bias taking place.

It seems like social media may be a major threat to the future of marriage, as never before in human history have we had this unprecedented access to all of our former lovers' latest photos and contact information.

One click is all it takes to feed the addiction. So ensure that you stay clean and keep moving forward. Let them lure themselves back into the trap by making yourself a scarce mystery that they can secretly project all of their futures dreams onto.

CHAPTER 10

Long Distance Breakups

Long-distance relationships are very much a modern phenomenon. Before the wonders of air travel, mobile phones and Wifi, it used to be that when a loved one had to move away to another country, they hopped on a boat and it was 'Goodbye forever'. A tear would be shed, but you would simply live with the pain and mystery of what could have been. But nowadays, we do not allow a petty detail like living in another country and not physically getting to spend time with your significant other to get in the way of a potential future together. Ironically the internet has brought the world much closer together in this respect. You can travel freely and even move to a new city or country for work while staying in contact with loved ones, but it comes at a heavy cost. While technology gives us the illusion of everyone being closer together, our interpersonal relationships drift further and further apart.

We allow ourselves to take the shortcut of sending simple texts as opposed to meeting a friend in person. When we go to social gatherings, we spend the duration of our time there staring at our phone or waiting for an opportunity to do so. We are all addicted. So it's only natural that if your loved one has to move far away, a small voice inside you may suggest, '*Well, who cares? Monday to Friday is dominated by work anyway. And at the weekend we can either Skype or visit one another from the comfort of our own home. This can work. As long as we stay in constant contact, we may barely even notice the distance. I love you and I am not going to let this go or I won't be able to live with myself.*'

And in many respects that is a beautiful sentiment. Two people are so spellbindingly in love that nothing will get in the way. Being in a long-distance relationship is sentimentally one of the most passionate and romantic declarations you can make to one another. But unfortunately, the long-distance relationship itself is one of the least passionate, most frustrating experiences that causes your romantic connection to slowly pull itself apart limb by limb.

Of course there are many different types of long-distance. Some couples meet online and have never lived in the same city. These relationships are definitely in the minority. For most, two people meet one another at both the exact right time and the exact wrong time. They meet and their blossoming romance captivates a part of their imagination they never thought possible before. Their love ignites and carries them through a honeymoon period and beyond. It becomes impossible to imagine a life without this person. But life has other plans. One of you will have to move away to another city or country, typically against your will. This may be a job transfer, a college course, visa issues. The distance may be a two-hour drive or a ten-hour flight across the world, but however far it is or whatever the reason may be, an external factor has come into play and disrupted your future plans.

Both people in the relationship then come to a crossroads and a life-defining decision needs to be made. Will we break up or try long-distance? Some will dive head-first into long-distance, but most will contemplate the decision for a while with logical concerns like, *'How will this possibly work?'* They have likely never heard of a long-distance relationship working out before. They may have never even heard of someone trying long-distance before. They ask their friends and family and they either advise against it, or they are highly skeptical about this decision.

But the connection is too strong to let go of. So they ignore all logic and reason and decide that they are going to make long-distance work. This decision usually changes the person's mindset from, "I will *try* long-distance" to "I will *make* long-distance work" as they now realize they are all-in. If they don't fully believe that this deeply unlikely situation will work out, then it has no chance at all. So in a way, entering long-distance requires the participants to delude themselves into believing that this will work, because the anxiety of it not working out is an existential threat to the relationship itself. This causes circular reasoning, and when tested about the long-term viability of this relationship, the participants feel an immediate need to dismiss other people's opinions and skepticism. They re-enforce to themselves that this will all work out, because, akin to a cult member, they have faith and that's all that matters.

In some ways, the obstacle itself can be seen as romantic. You are both going to overcome the impossible and when you tell this story at your fiftieth wedding anniversary celebration, there won't be a dry eye in the house.

So you embark on your long-distance relationship with the best of intentions. You stay in contact as often as possible, and perhaps even schedule weekly Skype sessions. Video chats are usually viewed as the best way to feel closer together as you can both see and hear your partner. All you are missing out on is smell and touch. But secretly, neither of you actually enjoy the Skype sessions because it's almost like torture to see the person you love behind the prison of a screen, and it reminds you how they're not really there. Your internet connection can suffer, causing delays in conversation. Over time, this internet connection starts to become a symbol of your personal connection too. This highlights the uncomfortable reality that they are far, far away.

Can long-distance relationships work? Yes. If you have been together in-person for a long time. Longer than you will have to endure the long-distance period. And also if the long-distance is just be a period. Not forever. There needs to be a set timeline in which the distance will be resolved and you can both be back closer together again. If there is no guarantee that this long-distance will stop in the near-distant future, then there is no goal to aim for, so your time apart feels interminable and futile. This is why the overwhelming majority of long-distance relationships will fail. But unfortunately, for one or both people involved, they have delusionally convinced themselves that long-distance can work. It just takes grit, determination and true love. This often means that when the breakup occurs, this failure feels like a personal failure, as opposed to a circumstantial inevitability.

Think about it. What is a relationship? A commitment to one another, sure, but it's also based on you both spending quality time together, relying on one another, having fun together and embracing physical romantic activity. But in a long-distance relationship, you basically decide that you will both keep the commitment part... but cut 90% of the rest. Almost like you are stripping away vital organs from the relationship to see what the bare minimum requirement is to survive.

After a few months, the cracks usually start to show. Until now, you have remained in constant contact, mostly so you can convince one another that reality isn't happening. Your constant text updates, photo sharing and video chats are all to give the illusion of being by one another's side. Almost like, *'See, we're really doing this, we're basically still in the same room, this is totally normal!'* But after a while, you become just like another app on your partner's phone, not a romantic partner they can see or touch.

This is why long-distance relationships are almost impossible to sustain. Due to time differences and being in different cities, it feels as if you are living different lives. Because in reality, you are. There's just a part of you that is still mentally living in another city. Neither of you are happy and always consumed with your phone. A lot of your friends probably wish you weren't in a long-distance relationship and almost everyone around you tells you that they *"don't think they could ever do it"*, and you secretly know that really means they don't think it will work. This causes a low lying level of stress to reverberate around your subconscious constantly, knowing that your happiness is just one logical decision away from ending.

You have high hopes, but the problem is, reality keeps getting in the way of your plans. Everything that goes wrong in your life is made worse by the distance. Tired? Anxious? Horny? Lonely? All of this is made worse by your loved one not being anywhere close. Because long-distance is so hard, small problems become big problems, everything is under a microscope. You start to realize that you are living in a mere compromise, just trying not to lose one another. But the truth is, neither of you are fully happy… and that is unsustainable long term.

This is where the dumper and dumpee begin to mentally pull in different directions. One of you will eventually start experiencing the relationship killer; **Doubt**. The dumper starts sobering up from the crazy intense passion of your past romance and starts getting realistic. They ask themselves tough questions that increasingly lead them to the same conclusion. *'Do I see this lasting a year? 2 years? 10 years?'* They do this because on some level, they already know they have lost faith in this relationship working out and now they are experiencing confirmation bias. It becomes impossible for them to come up with reasons that this will work because that delusional, powerful, motivating love that they felt at the start, (usually prior to the distance being implemented) has faded. Now they start to feel as if they are neglecting their present tense happiness for a dream in the future that may never come to fruition. They want to stop living in the future, wondering if and when, and start building plans based in the here and now.

They are still attracted to you. They just despise the distance. So they may want you, but they can't have you without the distance... therefore, they decide that they need to stop wanting you too. This becomes easier for them because the distance has likely taken a toll on your mental health and your connection has weakened. So they start to pull away. They become less responsive and less enthusiastic about the relationship. Making future plans to meet in person becomes more challenging. It feels as if they are intentionally putting roadblocks in place. This behavior is a clear symptom that they do not see a future with you, so they are unwilling to commit to fully "trying" anymore. A part of them secretly hopes you will start to see that this just isn't working anymore, because they wish you were both on the same page.

But sadly, the dumpee's anxiety kicks in and they can see they run the risk of losing their partner. So while the dumper is trying to detach from this painful situation, no longer believing that this future utopia really exists, the dumpee is brainwashing themselves with the original manifesto more and more. Believing that they need to have their arguments for staying together absolutely straight if they're going to convince their partner to stay. This is no different than any cult member trying to stop their fellow believers from leaving the religion.

Unfortunately, this behavior typically drives the dumper further away and they become resolute in the decision. They cannot join your delusion, they have to participate in reality as it just makes more sense to them now. They're still upset about the decision and they know that on some level they will always wonder 'what if' but it becomes a necessary sacrifice for their mental health and future happiness.

After a long-distance breakup, it is vitally important that the dumpee starts no contact as soon as possible. This includes looking at the dumper's social media. Why? A painful consequence of being in a long-distance relationship is that you have started to get used to thinking about your partner even when they are not there. It's as if they live rent-free in your heart and mind. This makes the breakup earth-shattering, because while trying long-distance the dumpee has been totally ignoring their immediate surroundings and neglecting their present tense happiness, in exchange for participating in an online relationship in a city or country they don't actually live in. In a way, if you were the one who had to move away for whatever reason, and your relationship together existed back in your ex's city, then you have mentally not really arrived in your city yet. You are still mentally living in the other city because that is where you have memories with your partner, so you don't want to engage in your immediate surroundings or allow yourself to become fully happy. You do this because you know that if you become happy without your partner, then you run the risk of not giving your all to the relationship, or worse, giving up yourself.

So it is important that after the breakup is done, you do not chase after the dumper. They know all your reasons for wanting to stay together. But they have lost faith in long-distance, which is currently all you can offer. It is important to note that unless you cheated on them, no matter what the dumper said as the reason for breaking up, the real reason is the long-distance. There is no escaping that. *A loss of attraction?* Well yeah, because you are long-distance so they can't maintain physical attraction for someone who is not physically there. *Don't see a future with you?* Yes, as you are long-distance and there is either no end in sight, or they just can't imagine what the next step would look like as you have been apart for so long. Even if they leave you for someone else, guess why? It's because you aren't even there. So as tough as it is, try not to take it personally. This is a breakup with the situation, more than it is a breakup with you.

And that is what is so tough to accept for the dumpee. Because most of the time, the breakup happens in the same way your relationship has been for the last few months; over text, over the phone, or through a video chat. So it feels like it's not a real breakup because it didn't happen in person. It leaves behind a huge sense of unfinished business. The dumpee felt so powerless in the breakup because they were not there, so the urge to fight for the relationship lingers in the subconscious for a lot longer, because just like the relationship had stopped existing in physical reality, they did not get a chance to physically make their case and connect with the dumper one last time.

The dumpee believes that if the dumper could just see them in person, hear their voice, or kiss their lips, that all would be restored. This is often what drives the dumpee to make a grand gesture, like jumping in the car or buying a plane ticket, then turning up on the dumper's doorstep with a romantic speech prepared (that they've been drafting in their mind ever since the breakup conversation). But this is very unlikely to work because the dumper and the dumpee are psychologically existing in different realities.

The story in the dumper's mind is that long-distance does not work, the connection is gone and they cannot conceive of continuing any longer. The story in the dumpee's mind is that long-distance has taken a toll but the connection is still too strong to give up. This highlights that long-distance is the key issue.

But if you show up on the dumper's doorstep, you are likely justifying this behavior because you know long-distance is not working. So you logically conclude that if you show up in person then the distance is gone. Problem solved. But in reality, it's almost like you're doing this as a party trick. *"Ta-da, it didn't work while I was far away but now I am here!"*

But even if you simply keep texting or calling, the dumper will resist because their biggest fear after such a painful and shocking (yet brave) breakup decision, is being sucked back into a long-distance situation. Remember, they have just learned that this does not work long-distance so they don't want to re-enter any relationship in which long-distance is still in play as a possibility. Otherwise they feel that this will just happen again in a few weeks or months and they are too emotionally exhausted to engage with that fear.

Just like the name suggests, long-distance breakups take *longer* to get back together. They likely require playing the long game. Mostly because the emotional process of leaving a long-distance situation is unique. Initially, the dumper will likely also have a complete meltdown, tormented by what could have been, confused by this separation anxiety from someone who has not even been in the room with them for a long time. But after that, there is an undeniable feeling of incomparable freedom. They are no longer committed to someone who is not there, so they will feel a large sense of relief for a while afterwards.

The good news is that long-distance relationships are so crazy that they do leave behind a sense of unfinished business and comradery. It's almost like you both fought side-by-side in the same war, and no one else around them could ever understand. They will likely never try to do long-distance again with anyone else because the key lesson they learned here is that long-distance does not work. This means that long-distance exes usually do reconnect at some point in the future, simply out of desire for closure, or curiosity about what happened to that person they did that insane thing with once.

So, what to do if and when they do contact you. This is challenging because you cannot simply meet up with the person and you don't want to risk becoming occasional pen-pal friends. If it's a text, respond to their texts with texts... not a call. When you do, make it fun and positive (not too flirty right away or you are over-eager).

Assuming you are still long-distance then you should be the one to end the interaction. Politely excuse yourself because you are busy or meeting up with friends or doing an activity. That way you are demonstrating that your ex is not a priority to you anymore. It also highlights that unlike when you were in the long-distance relationship, you are no longer neglecting your immediate surroundings. That you have a life outside of this interaction and they can't just expect you to be readily available all the time. Things have changed now thanks to their decision. This will also leave them wanting more.

If you both end up texting more, then one day if they text you, call them back. You can justify this by claiming you are driving or that you're walking somewhere so you can't text. It is an excuse, but at this point, you are past the point of texting and they are initiating contact with you. This builds momentum and feels as if you are graduating to new phases of your relationship again. Hearing someone's voice is far more intimate than just texting words. Think of it as unlocking new levels. No Contact is now over, but you need to keep the ratio around 80/20 of them contacting you first, so they don't feel smothered, as yet again, their big fear is being sucked back into a long-distance relationship.

If calls are going well, you could just suggest meeting up as it would be good to actually see one another in person again. But there can be no pressure for a relationship. They have to feel as if this is a casual reconnection, not a commitment renegotiation.

But again, the dumper is uncertain about this whole situation and avoiding getting back together. Remember that they do not want to go backwards, ever, they want to go forwards. Pressure is the enemy of uncertainty and they currently host a lot of uncertainty about you and this situation. So the pressure of you both choosing to meet up together again could cause them to resist (unless they are already back saying 'I love you' on the phone or you live relatively close by).

But if you are far far away; many hours drive or a plane ride away, then you need to make meeting up as easy as possible for the dumper. You want them to feel this is actually very convenient or almost "like fate". When in conversation, drop in the idea of one of you visiting the other person's city for reasons that are unrelated to simply just seeing one another.

For example, you are being sent to their city for a work conference for a few days. Or you are going to a music festival or visiting your friends. Or if that does not work, then suggest that you recently went to an amazing concert or a museum or show (something that is in line with their interests) in your city and they would have loved it and you recommend they visit to check it out. See how they react...

Talk about it briefly, but whether they seem interested or not, you do the same thing next...

Nothing!

Not yet. They must be the one to bring it up again in the future before you book any flights or make plans. This is how you see actual interest. You suggest something then they confirm it. Otherwise, they could feel as if you are steering too intensely which causes them to back away if they aren't ready. It also will make you anxious that they didn't ever express enough mutual interest beyond a first impression. And that will make you feel as if you are pressing the action and perhaps making a fool of yourself with your big gesture.

The reason you just drop the idea in and await their future confirmation, is that you have now given them a mental crutch to lean on. Now you can gauge their interest level by when they bring it up again. Rather than saying "I miss you" or "I want to see you", they will lean on, "When are you coming to visit for that conference/festival/trip again?" It makes it easy for them and they feel as if there is less pressure on the trip as you have an ulterior motive and they are under less pressure to face the reality that they may be setting themselves up for future reconciliation. Remember, they do not want to feel as if they are going backwards, so they will likely lie to themselves about why they are meeting up with you. Fine. Let them. All that matters is that they reached out and now a future plan exists to casually see each other again and have a good time together.

After that, either they visit your city or you visit theirs. You obviously meet up, and see how it goes. It's highly likely you will hook up as this is giving you both reminders of what you used to be like together in person. It's a shock to the system. And tends to bring back all those memories and feelings you have tethered to that person. Just like how when you see an old friend, you tend to mimic that same social dynamic you used to have together no matter how long has passed. People tend to fall back into the usual habits they have with a person. Certain people unlock a unique aspect of your personality. This causes certain things to feel a lot more possible with some people than they do with others. This is why all former lovers spending time alone together is always a very high risk for romance re-emerging. And being in person changes everything in long-distance, as long as both people are receptive to it.

If you're going to bring up the relationship and what went wrong, do so after you have sexually or physically bonded again. You want to both test-drive the romance again first and allow the natural dopamine rush to flourish.

You should never start with a commitment negotiation... but once you are vibing and warmed up, then you can discuss what went wrong. But always make sure that you frame the breakup as an inevitable consequence of long-distance not working. That is the story of your breakup. Not a lack of connection between you both. They will agree with you, as that is the conclusion everyone comes to in these situations unless there is a glaring other reason, and they have also just reconnected with you romantically with no pressure so they have no evidence that your connection is an issue.

Now, this is the tricky part... you will need a realistic plan to close the distance within a certain time period. If you do not close the distance, I will tell you this right now... you will fail again. There is no point in getting back into the same relationship again if the same problem remains. There is no point in saying one more spin on the merry-go-round for old times sakes. Because once the second breakup happens... That is it. They are done and they won't re-engage the idea as they will consider it a lesson harshly learned that they didn't need to learn again. So you should have a realistic plan with practical solutions and a reasonable timeline in place. Be realistic, not reactive. It is easier to sign up for an unpressurized plan with real solutions, as opposed to a daydream that's centered around having faith and believing super-duper hard this time.

Long-distance breakups always leave a huge sense of unfinished business for everyone involved. It leaves a big question mark, a *what-if...* but that question mark is not about whether or not they could make long-distance work. The question mark is about what would have happened if the distance was never an issue in the first place?

So there needs to be a clear and realistic way that this can become a reality or you are setting yourself for an unnecessary sequel.

There are of course other options with long-distance. If you end up moving back to the city you lived in with your ex, and they still live there, then this is a total **gamechanger**. You should not contact them right away when you arrive. That would be over-eager. You do not want them to think that you got off the plane or stepped out of the car and the first thing you thought of was them. As if they are a personal mission for you. Remember that if you are moving back to that city, it is likely months or years later. Time has passed. Things have changed.

You want to settle back into the city. Have a new place to live, a job, a lifestyle. Exist for a while so that you remind yourself that you enjoy this city independently and do not need your ex at all. After a few weeks or ideally months, when you are less invested and view them as just another potential option, then you can make minor advances to test the waters.

- Firstly, post on social media that you live in that city again when you arrive. They may secretly check your social media (over 55% of Americans still check their ex's social media according to a study by Superdrug)[8]. This gives them an opportunity to reach out.

- Secondly, join dating apps. Now that you are single and new to this city again, it is natural for you to date. Ensure that your profile is both subtle and clear that you live in this city again and are working. If they live locally, they may see you on the dating app and either choose to match with you again, or just take note of this and over time choose to reach out to you directly to see how you are doing.

- Thirdly, and I dislike this suggestion but I have seen it work, you can like a post on their social media to draw some attention to yourself. Then let them like a post of yours back or reach out to you directly after seeing you are back in town permanently.

- Lastly, if things were left amicably and mutually, and enough time has passed, ask a loyal friend to check your ex's social media to see if they are still single. If they do not appear to be dating anyone, then you can text them directly. Not call. But a lot of time would need to have passed and you would need to be settled into the city. This way your ex can see that you have a full life and are not just chasing them. Instead, you would now be similar to anyone else they would consider dating, as opposed to playing the role of their ex who wants them back. The only reason why this is a rare exception to breaking no contact is that you living in the same city again naturally (not just to get them back) is a gamechanger. And they may not have ever known or suspected you are now living there again.

Put no pressure on getting back together. Have a light back and forth with them. If they seem cold, back off with no pressure and let them contact you again. Don't invite them to meet up unless they seem very receptive. If they hint at meeting up or create clear opportunities for you to ask, then you can suggest it on the first interaction. But otherwise, it is best to let them reach out the next time to confirm mutual interest. Then you can ask them to meet up and it will feel natural. If you reach out and ask in the first exchange that may confirm an imbalance of interest. As they will be surprised to hear from you and if you are automatically pushing to meet up it may remind them of the breakup dynamic again and they will push away. They will be naturally cautious and suspicious, so instead, just let it be a fun, light, reconnection. Even a fun appreciative reflection on the good times. Afterwards, give them the space to wonder and reconsider. Let their subconscious do the work. If they are still interested and you left the last text exchange on a positive note, then they will think about you more. Attraction can grow in that space and they can simply contact you.

But aside from that, unless they are contacting you, demonstrating mutual interest, or behaving warmly, you are simply moving on and enjoying your new city again. If and when they are ready, they can contact you.

CHAPTER 11

Back in Contact

At this point, you have been in a state of no contact with your ex for some time, moving forward assuming it is permanent. You have let go, healed and started making genuine progress in your life. Your mind is no longer clenched like a fist holding onto the memories of the past. You feel rejuvenated, active and forward-looking. And then one day that starts like any other, you get a message on your phone. You expect it could be anyone; friends, family members, potential new romantic partners… but no, it's your ex. It catches you totally off guard and you don't know what to do or think. Why is the person who broke up with me suddenly back in contact?

Well, let's continue the story from the dumper's perspective. We have already established that at the time of the breakup, they experienced *self-doubt, confusion, and guilt*. They needed time and space away from you because they had been mounting pressure on themselves and this decision.

Once the breakup conversation is completed, they feel they need to achieve what they set out to do. They need to be independent and figure out who they are outside of that relationship and establish what it is they truly want. After all, they have just made a major decision, so they feel that some real changes are likely necessary. If the dumpee contacts them and interrupts this process by trying to convince to change their mind, this usually highlights to them that you are both on two different wavelengths and the more it happens, they may feel even more justified for ending a relationship with someone they are so blatantly incompatible with. But assuming that the dumpee does not chase for long or never chases, then No Contact begins.

Silence…

Relief.

It's over. Finally, some time to be alone with their thoughts.

Now with this newfound freedom, the first thing they'll do is go out, often drinking or partying with their friends. This is a natural response for anyone. It's a time to reconnect with friends and socialize. They are coming to terms with the reality that they are single now, and they likely told themselves this was the path forward that would bring them the most happiness. So they must now make their life exciting just like they told themselves it should be. Otherwise, what was the point in breaking up? But they also feel pressure to justify all of this breakup pain to themselves and the world. Keep in mind that friends and family are judging them for ending a relationship that other people still believed in. They claimed they wanted to be single, and now they are, so there is pressure to prove they did it for good reason.

This is why they will usually take to social media and post slightly strange photos of themselves online. Maybe it's a selfie to seek validation through likes. Maybe it's photos of them out partying with friends. Or a cryptic message about "life" and this "unexpected journey" they are on. Usually it conveys how great they are doing. A sort of, *"Look at me, I am out, it's fun. I'm fun. I'm rediscovering a whole part of myself I forgot about."* This is usually very upsetting for the dumpee, who feels like the dumper is rubbing it in their face in a conceited attempt to "win" the breakup.

But if they drink, they find themselves thinking about you when they are hungover or towards the end of the night. They will consider messaging you but don't want to risk upsetting you or accidentally leading you on. So they don't.

During this relief period, the dumper will force themselves into proactive social mode, arranging constant activities to do that will keep them busy and around friends. They don't like being alone with their thoughts like they did in the beginning. Now it's just lonely, and it makes them think about what happened; *how they hurt you, and how they hurt themselves too.*

But as time passes and life takes over, the friends that were totally available in the immediate aftermath of the breakup are gradually less and less available to hang out. Keep in mind these friends initially made themselves overly available to aid this painful transition for the dumper and to "be there" as any good friend should. They start to notice that you are still not contacting them at all. They start to wonder why not and occasionally tell themselves that it's probably okay for you both to be civil and say 'hi' once in a while. They don't recognize they are missing you fully yet, they justify these thoughts as mere self-reflection. They then take it a step further and start to look at your social media. They discover you're either not posting anything (making you a total mystery) or you seem totally fine and active. This is oddly not satisfying for them, as they are starting to admire your strength for not chasing after them. A small part of them wanted to see a series of tragic social media posts about being heartbroken and missing them.

They end up alone more. They wonder if you're alone. They then may decide it's time to date. Time to see what is out there. So they go on a date, but they don't really think they want a relationship as they are still wondering if there is something wrong with them as they felt guilty for losing faith in your relationship. But they know that they are single and they need to justify their actions to themselves. If they wanted to be single, then they should see what else is out there. But naturally, this new person they date isn't as familiar and doesn't have the same level of chemistry with them. They find themselves resorting to template language like, *'What do you do?'*, *'Any cool trips planned?'* or describing themselves as if they are in a job interview. It feels a little empty and like hard work.

Then they really start to wonder about you. They think about the relationship more and more. It's weird you haven't been chasing... but then they remind themselves they left you and they have no right to wonder. They check on your social media again and you're doing very well. You're thriving. They'll start getting the impression that you don't really need them anymore and you're just moving on, unlike them, who is currently stalking your life. They've gone from being the one leaving to the secret investigator. Nothing is more humbling than that. It's like quitting a job but still hoping for an invite to the Christmas party.

Now that the dust has settled, all those reasons for breaking up have run out of steam. The Fading Affect Bias is taking place, so they don't have the same emotional attachment to certain negative memories they once had. The past seems less relevant as they can see you're doing fine now. Painfully, you're doing better than them. They start feeling a little rejected back. They start to wonder; *Do you still care about me? Are you dating someone new? What have you realized about me that's caused you to not reach out anymore? Will others start to realize the same thing?*

They respect you now. And quietly resent when others ask about you or how they are coping with the breakup. Because they have no idea how you are and they assume you are handling the breakup better than them.

But one day they either officially decide or spontaneously find themselves messaging you. Just something simple. A 'how are you'. They will convince themselves; *'What's the harm? We knew each other for a long time. We can be friends, right? I mean obviously not friends as you specifically said no to that, but we can talk, we used to talk all the time. Maybe I'll just see if you're angry or okay. Maybe you'll want me back right away and be desperate. That would be awful (but kind of not really as that is the status quo).'*

They have no idea what to expect, but that's when they contact you. Just an innocent little message. And now they wait for your response... anxiously... beginning to wonder if you are even going to reply. Because you could not and that would be totally justified.

And then you do... and relief washes over them. They lean in towards their phone with focus. If their last point of contact with you was the breakup, then they will be experiencing similar levels of anxiety now because it feels like a continuation of the previous dialogue.

From your side of things, you may be totally over your ex and not even instinctively want them back. That is a real possibility. Either way, you are likely going to look at the message in complete disbelief. For weeks or months (or sometimes years) you have likely been anticipating how it would feel to receive the perfect message. That they reach out begging for you to take them back right away. It's almost like a secret little evil plan of yours. To force the person who rejected you to come crawling back. You'll feel powerful, validated and vindicated. Muhahaha.

But— It's unlikely to go that way. As disappointing as it is, most exes do not reach out asking to get back together right away. So you may feel a little disappointed with how innocuous the message appears to be. Communication is a funny thing, because on the face of it, it can appear like nothing at all. But **subtext, backstory** and **behavior** all have to be taken into account.

The subtext of what is being said is vitally important. If someone you have not spoken to in a long time messages you a simple, *'How are you?'* then when you factor in the backstory and the behavior to the message, then the real subtext of the message is, *'I have been thinking about you'* or *'I miss you'*. Because why else would someone you are not in regular contact with reach out to you? They are curious about you, they're thinking about you, and they want you to know that they are and reconnect with you.

You can factor in other details too. If you receive a

message at 3 am on a Saturday morning then the likelihood is that they are intoxicated or emotionally exhausted, both of which can make people more honest and less risk-averse.

Every villain is a hero in their own mind. Most dumpers do not think they are on any level moving towards getting back together. Because that would mean they were wrong to end the relationship. And most of us don't believe we were totally wrong, almost ever. Because we know that we rationalized our decision to do what we did. We are living within that story. And this is what is important to understand about what to do when an ex reaches out. It's not about proving them wrong, it's not about confronting them, it's about building a bridge from the story they were living in back then, to the story you want them to live in now.

Dumpers are human, and they want to protect themselves first and foremost. Their opening message may not be very satisfying on the surface, but the behavior speaks for them. In that moment they are breaking no contact because they cannot take it anymore.

Let's decode some of the subtext and backstory in the messages they may send:

Very positive contact:

- "I miss you" = They're feeling weak and want you to reciprocate to soothe their anxiety

- "Remember that amazing/funny time we…" = They want to mentally place you back in a memory they can't seem to forget

- "You look great/beautiful/handsome/fit/strong in your new photo" = They want you to know they still find you attractive

- "Can we talk?" = I have been overthinking about something and I need to get it off my chest

Neutral-positive contact:

- "How are you?" = I miss you and I am curious but I don't want to admit that

- "Our mutual friend told me something great you did so I wanted to say congratulations" = I am impressed. Or I want you to know I still want the best for you.

- "What was *that* experience like?" = I saw you traveled somewhere new or did something cool and I am a little jealous, so I thought I'd use that as a springboard back into contact by using something positive. I am also impressed you're so active.

- "I saw something funny and I just decided to share it with you" = We usually enjoy the same things and I think we still do. Or I want to test if you will respond and this is the easiest way I can think of with minimal risk because you'll respond about the content, not me personally.

Neutral contact:

- "I am just checking in" = I was clearly thinking about you but I don't want you to think I am leading you on. Don't chase me.

- "I thought you should know about news regarding my pet/asking about your pet" = I can't ask you how you are, so I'll talk about the pet instead to see if you respond. We can also then discuss our affection for the pets instead of talking directly.

- "There is an event on soon I think may interest you" = I saw this and thought of you, I'm not ready for real conversation yet.

- "Happy Birthday/Merry Christmas" = Here is your generic message that I did not put much thought into, but wanted to keep things civil. Don't overreact.

Nothing to get excited about contact:

- "I have some of your stuff you might want" = I don't want to be rude but I do want to tie up all loose ends

- "Here is your mail" = Please stop having your mail addressed to my house

Whenever you are back in contact with an ex, it is important to not overreact or show too much interest. If they are breaking no contact after a long period of time you should never go over-the-top with your responses. This means that if they write three words: 'How are you?' You should not write back a twelve sentence essay mapping out your precise emotional state coupled with a checklist of the progress you've made.

On some level, every dumper anxiously anticipates that you will just start re-reading from the same script as the breakup again no matter what they say. The most common mistake I have seen throughout my email advice is that when an ex reaches out, the dumpee immediately starts talking about the breakup. Either saying they want to meet up to "talk" or trying to renegotiate the commitment while firmly repeating their frantic disagreement with the original breakup decision. Or else they try to make the dumper feel guilty for how miserable they have felt without them.

Remember, your ex already felt guilty when they were breaking up with you. Now you have had time apart. You want to show them that you are in a different headspace, not still stuck in that mental loop. The reason most dumpees fall into this trap is because firstly, it's what they want, so their anxiety doesn't want to waste another second not addressing the bleeding wound in their chest. But secondly, it's because human beings tend to pick up where they left off with one another. If your last conversation was highly emotional, then seeing that person is going to place you back to that time and place, and you'll feel those same piping hot emotions. So the dumpee often gets the contact they've been seeking, but in that moment they almost can't differentiate between the past and present, so they just continue where they left off... the breakup.

This is why I say, if you want to reattract the dumper then you need to act based on their needs and divert their expectations, as opposed to satisfying your immediate anxious impulses.

What do they need? The dumper ended the relationship and in that moment they felt justified in their decision because they believed it would be best for both of you. If you keep trying to dig back into the past to prove them wrong, then you will get nowhere and are missing the fundamental principle of getting back together with an ex; **you are moving forward, not backward.** No one wants to feel as if they are taking a step backwards in life. So if they feel they were right to have broken up with you because the trajectory of your relationship felt negative, then the right approach does not involve bitterness or disagreement. Rather, you should seem as if your life is a moving train they can hop on board.

If they see you are not talking about the past, are active in your present, and moving towards a more prosperous future, then it seems more like the breakup was beneficial for both of you, and you on some level agree that (at the time) it was the right choice.

This also eliminates their feelings of guilt, which is vitally important for reattraction. If you are the victim of the breakup, then they feel guilty for hurting you. But if you seem to be so at peace that you spiritually understand and agree with their decision, then you are not enemies on different teams, you are on the same team, and therefore, equals. It also allows them to not have to consider their previous decision a big mistake which resolves a lot of inner conflict. If they can maintain the original story in their mind (that they made the right choice) then they are on the right path with you.

This does not mean that you believe you were entirely to blame for the breakup. Nor should you tell them directly that they were totally right and you don't belong together. But simply that you seem at peace and hold no grudges. You don't bring up the past breakup and are more focused on what you've done since and what you've learned. If you hold no grudge and both seem to be getting along in the present tense, then it is easier for them to picture a future with you. Whereas if you are bitter, angry or upset, then you are living in the past and appear to have made no progress.

By disagreeing with their past decision, you make them defensive and this launches you both back into conflict. This can feel good for the dumpee to get it out of their system and they can often feel they deserve to hurt the dumper. However, this actually fuels them through the breakup even more, as now they have a fresh reminder about why you don't function together anymore. So instead, shift focus away from the bad experiences of the past onto the present positives. This way it refreshes their memory. The dumper can then re-frame the story of you in their own mind, not as a tragedy or a sympathetic character, but someone strong, attractive and competent.

Now when it comes to what to say, I'm not going to tell you specific quotes, because if I do you will be rigid and stick to someone else's script, which is unnatural for you. I often see people copy and paste in certain quotes they have been told to say by dating experts word-for-word and it never reads well in the cold light of day. Remember, you are yourself. You are the person that attracted your ex in the first place. Context and momentum matter for all forms of contact, so you will need to be yourself and wing it to an extent. Any quotes I do provide, feel free to adapt or change them to your own tone of voice. This may be scary as you are anxious and feel like you are defusing a bomb, but it's also the only way for you to do the job correctly without it seeming out of character. But I will advise you on what not to do.

As we discussed, be light and fun and seem totally unphased about the breakup. Talk in the present and future tense. Do not bring up the past, commitment or the breakup. Do not reply with walls of text— that is a bad first impression. We want you both to feel like you have mutual interest as opposed to them having a first impression that you are too invested due to the length of your response. If they ask a quick question via text, responding with a handwritten letter communicates you are far too invested. Write shorter messages that mirror the size of theirs. Remember, **mirror their interest level**. If they write something long, then you indulge in a longer message. If they write a sentence, then they get a sentence back. If they wait a while to respond, don't get anxious and double text.

As the contact unfolds, try to read the room a little. **Test their temperature**. If they are responding fast and seem engaged, then they are warm. If they never ask any questions or respond with minimal effort a few hours later, then they are cold. Mirror that and don't be afraid to stop responding. The most common mistake I see at this stage is the dumpee getting anxious and rewarding cold behavior with an invitation to meet up. Usually this is because they have heard they should always invite the dumper out if they contact. But you want to test their temperature first so that you do not dive head-first into a swimming pool with no water in it. If they are willing to meet up, then they are willing to message a little bit first, right? But if the dumper responds with conversation closers like, "Cool", "Thanks", or "No prob", then this is not the time to panic and go all-in with an invitation to meet up. If the conversation has not been engaging or warm, then this will make them feel like, *'Why would I meet up with you to do this in person? It's not even that fun over text?'*

This is why I recommend you have a light back and forth first, to cleanse the palate and build some momentum. When the conversation is at a peak (perhaps they are laughing at a little joke, or at a time when both of you appear to be engaged, reactive and responding fast), this is the time to ask to "Catch up properly in person." This is the most natural time to ask, as it feels like, *'This is fun, why not? We're already having a good time.'*

Now, they may so no. This is natural, they may not be ready yet and are still living in the story that they chose to end it so don't think it would be right to meet up. Fine. Simply tell them: *"Cool, let me know if you change your mind"*. This way if they were expecting an overreaction, they do not get one, and they can reach out again next time. It is vitally important not to ***pressure*** your ex to meet up. They must be mutually interested. Remember that pressure is the enemy of uncertainty and they currently host a lot of uncertainty about you. When pressured, people tend to default back to their original position because it's the safest option.

If they say yes, great, suggest meeting up for drinks in the evening, not daytime. The reason being that going for drinks is fun but also allows for an easy excuse to get loose and make mistakes. Sometimes people like to fall back on the excuse that "they were drunk". This is mere self-protection. You don't need to drink alcohol at all, but just ensure that it seems like a casual fun way to spend time together. The reason you should suggest the night time is that in the daytime we feel more responsible as we can be fully seen, whereas psychologically the night is when risks are taken in the cloak of darkness. It's as if God has gone to sleep and no one can be judged for their sins. Being out late at night is a much better situation than going for a quick coffee on a Tuesday afternoon like they're a distant relative. Don't get me wrong, coffee *can* work, but it's usually quick and innocent, jammed in between other real plans.

The dumper may resist the invitation and ask for qualifiers like, *'Is this just as friends?'* When they ask this, it's usually a cautious kneejerk response because they would like to see you, but they also like the comfort of living in the story that they are not changing their mind or going backwards. The problem is that if you tell them that you want to meet just as friends, then you have semi-castrated yourself, and if you make a move on them, you are in the wrong for misleading them. So how to dodge this uncomfortable question...

If you're super confident and generally sarcastic, then you can play around a little and suggest, *"Haha sure, totally just friends"*. But this may make them anxious and they will reassert that they are serious and refuse to go without further confirmation. So that is only for rare, hyper-confident, positive situations.

For most, it is best to simply create a grey area between just being friends, and this being a meet up between two former lovers. Remind them that *"you have too much chemistry to <u>ever really</u> just be friends but it would be fun to catch up anyway"*. This way you don't accept friendship but you justify your reasons with the reality that you have a romantic history. This on some level communicates that you can't just be friends because you get along too well. It's important to not slip into negative talk, so reminding them that the only "problem" is that you both get on too well is a better strategy. You also then shrug it off as it would just be fun to see them. This makes them feel they are being a stick in the mud for not going as the chat has been light and fun so far.

Their last qualifier will usually be asking for confirmation that this is not a date. Reassure them that, *"No it's a catch up"*. This way you have not called it a date, but not accepted friendship, so you exist in limbo, just like your current relationship status. Despite you not calling it a date, they are aware of your romantic history and likely do suspect this could go somewhere. Especially if alcohol is involved. They know they are taking a risk, and the sexual tension of not knowing what may happen is appealing. Whereas "meeting up to talk about us" is not fun, it's predictable and likely leads to a repeat of the breakup conversation.

Breadcrumbs:

A lot of dumpees hope that the dumper breaks no contact and reaches out one day. For others, they can't seem to get them to stop. Some dumpers stay in contact all the time with pointless bits and pieces of contact here and there. These are called ***breadcrumbs***. They keep you interested and can sometimes feel like they're leading somewhere, but they never do. Typically what happens is that the dumper reaches out but then refuses to meet up for whatever reason. They then continue to stay in contact now and then. They send links to funny videos and news articles or ask pointless questions about your friends and family, yet never want to meet up. This frustrates the dumpee and they don't know what to do.

If they keep sending pointless breadcrumbs, then you can just stop responding to those unless there is something of real substance coming in. This does not mean you ignore their original messages, but if the conversation never goes anywhere worthwhile, then you can just stop responding at a certain point. This way you stop rewarding the breadcrumb messages with a response, which disincentivizes them to keep sending those kinds of messages. This way they have to alter their behavior to get a response from you, which altars their current pattern of thinking about you too.

Or you can simply confront it and politely cut them off. This way they feel a little rejected back. It is totally fair to say, '*Look, I've been thinking about it… you and I have too much history to just be text buddies like this, so I don't think we can continue casually messaging if we're not even considering meeting up*'. If they disagree then you can reason them out of it, while revealing your mindset; '*Yeah… I just don't think it makes sense. If I start dating someone or you start dating someone, then they will not be cool with us staying in contact like this*'. Now you have planted in their mind that you are going to start moving on now, which makes them face the loss and recognize that there are consequences to their decision.

If they contact again after this point, be warm so that you reward that courageous decision, then ask them to meet up because it would be good to see them. Do not address their feelings, as the behavior is likely telling you more than they are comfortable voicing.

Hot and Cold Behavior:

But what if your ex is back in contact, yet giving you unpredictable ***hot and cold behavior*** on the phone? This can be endlessly frustrating because they appear hot by exchanging warm conversation, seeming really engaged... but then they don't answer for five days. Or when you ask them out, they go cold... or worst-case scenario, don't even reply. So what should you do?

Simply, you don't pursue any further. Back to no contact. A lot of the time your anxiety may take over and you start messaging too much to try to secure the date. But by doing so you are showing that you need it too much, and thus, have not really changed since the breakup conversation. You need to need the relationship slightly less than them, so don't overpursue or reward this negative behavior.

Let them come to you again. When they do the next time, if it's going well... rather than following the previous pattern of behavior by asking them to meet, instead, you be the one to end the conversation as you have other priorities. Just keep it fun, light, short and sweet, then exit positively, telling them, "*talk to you soon*". Then let them be the ones to initiate contact again.

Why do this? Firstly, because you don't need to get burned twice in a row. That's a bad trend to set. But secondly, because they are getting too comfortable. They are playing with their food. They need to see that you don't need them and are not going to prioritize them if they burn you like this. It's all about rewarding positive behavior, like reaching out, and disincentivizing negative behavior, like not responding and rejecting you. Then, if and when they reach out again a third time, you can hint at meeting up.

So that's hot and cold behavior on the phone, but what about in person? Sometimes it can happen that the plan seems to be going perfectly. They break no contact, you message one another, invite them out, have drinks, catch up, make lingering eye contact and it goes so well that you end up sleeping together.

Then they back off unexpectedly. A generous interpretation could be that they got cold feet about where this was going and decided it was a mistake. So simply mirror their interest level and back away too.

But then if they reach out again and they seem hot; texting, flirting, but it's just sexual stuff, then this may be turning into a Friends with Benefits situation.

If you're a stereotypical man, then this may initially work for you as a way of rebuilding the connection over time (although there should be consistency and/or building momentum or you are just helping her wean off you slowly).

But if you're a woman, then you need to be careful not to just reward the man with sex any time he messages you. You're not a booty call. That is a major demotion from being in a relationship.

Whatever gender you are, if it seems they only want a Friends with Benefits situation... that might be nice, but it's likely that after all this rejection that this will not be a healthy decision for you. So simply meet up for drinks again the next time but don't sleep with them.

The problem can be that if they are behaving hot and cold, you are more likely to try to give them as much as possible in an attempt to win them back. But that does not test their interest at all. You can be romantic together but you do not need to reward their behavior of going cold by sleeping with them every time. If you don't have sex with them and then they disappear forever then you now know their true intentions. You should not feel interchangeable with a one night stand.

But sometimes you have the opposite problem. If you and your ex are exchanging hot flirty messages and it seems like momentum is building. They want you. And you want them. Or so it seems... because then when you meet, a revolting surprise awaits... they are no longer hot or romantic. They were talking about cuddling, having you next to them, but when you meet you try something sexual and they insist 'no'.

What are they doing? Well, they could just be helping themselves get over you. They are likely not aware they are doing this. We tell ourselves many stories and play many games, even with ourselves. They wanted to see you, but still don't know if this is a bad idea, so instead, they decide to simply suck some attention out of you in order to aid their separation anxiety. This can be a cruel twist of fate.

So what do you do?

The key is being less readily available, and while they are acting hot towards you, occupying more of their time and space in their mind. Instead of rushing over to their house instantly because they hinted that they might want a cuddle, linger in that mental spot for longer. Attraction can grow in that space. Sometimes the most fun part of a kiss is the anticipation of it right before it happens when your faces are right next to one another. That focus. That desire. That lust. That's what you want to create here.

If they suggest they want you to come over and "cuddle", respond but keep the focus on how nice it *would* be, and how maybe you *could* come over, but you're not sure. Tease them a little. Ask them how would it feel? Get them talking about what they want, how they want it, and what they like about it. Remember, they're the ones coming to you warm. You don't need to rush over there like a horny teenager.

You're a competent and confident functioning member of society. You have other priorities and responsibilities. Tell them you have work and you're hoping maybe you can get out early, but you're not sure. Have them try to lure you away from your other tasks.

While they're tempting you, they are now mentally playing that role, they are starting to fight for you. They are now trying to convince you to turn them into your priority again. Do you see? This is how you turn the tables slowly and let them feel as if they are pursuing you. Once they are, the breakup and who-broke-up-with-who is a distant memory.

What you focus on, grows, so let them focus on the idea of you coming over for longer. Don't be afraid to delay gratification. The best things can be worth waiting for.

If they keep being hot and cold or rejecting offers then make yourself a challenge to them. If they want to be unpredictable and hot and cold, then you tame that by feeding their impulses, but not giving it any gratification.

Let them go crazy trying to convince you, while you try to slot them into your schedule. This puts them in your palm, returning the power and attraction to you. Stop trying to understand their fluctuating interest and start trying to captivate it, tame it and turn the tables so that they're almost getting you but not quite. This way, when they do, they never want to risk letting you go again.

Dating Other People:

Sometimes your ex gets back in contact with you but they are now openly ***dating someone new***. Maybe it's a rebound, maybe it's a serious relationship. Who knows. But they are openly dating someone else when they contact you. This is confusing because you likely thought they would never reach out to you while seeing someone else, but here we are.

Most dumpees will be so thrilled that their ex is contacting them that they will indulge the conversation for as long as possible. This can work and it seems logical. The strategy is clearly to start slowly luring the dumper away from this new person they are seeing. You feel a little evil, but you are in competitive mode, you just want to "win".

The problem is, oftentimes you just end up exhausting the conversation by talking for a few hours and then you run out of steam. They end up saying something like, *'Ok well it was good catching up, bye...'* and you stare at your phone in disbelief. *Is that it? Seriously what the fuck was that? How could you do this to me?* The reason this happens is that you have now satisfied their need for validation and their curiosity. They got their fill of you. They know exactly what is going on in your life and they know you still want them (sort of), so they don't need any more than that. It's selfish but they likely feel they were just being nice and reconnecting. They will never tell themselves they are the villain of the situation.

Others will nosedive straight into an invitation to meet up right away. The problem is that if they already have someone else in their life they will likely say 'no'. Additionally, by jumping to an invite, you are revealing how readily available you are while they are off exploring other options. This subconsciously communicates that you are on the sidelines waiting for them. That they are the prize.

In these situations, you have limited options. You can do anything, including just pretending that the new person doesn't exist and asking them out as if they are single. Fine.

But in my view, you don't want to reward someone for reaching out to you while they are openly dating someone else. You have to look beyond the initial relief that they are contacting and take a calculated risk.

If they are contacting their ex while in a new

relationship, then let's be honest, they are likely not very satisfied with this new person they are dating. Why? Because it's disrespectful and inconsiderate to be actively reaching out to a former lover while committed to someone else.

So if they aren't fully satisfied with what they have, then you should use reverse psychology and send them back to the very thing they are dissatisfied with, after dangling something better in front of their face.

Firstly, have a fun back and forth for a few minutes. Then when the conversation hits a little peak, rather than asking them to meet up (as they have a ready-made excuse that they can't as they are dating someone else), you cut the conversation short by saying something like: '*But anyway, I guess you shouldn't be texting me like this, as it's not fair on this new person.*'

Tone is important, you say this with no animosity and no vindictiveness. You're light about it, but you're also being the grown-up in the room. You're taking the high road. But what does this do? It achieves a lot with very little because of the backstory and baggage they are bringing into the situation.

- You lightly reject them back.

- They face consequences. They had a new lover and were texting their ex-lover, but now they just get one.

- You remind them that you both have sexual undertones when you interact and you aren't a normal person for them to message

- This makes your interactions a secret and thus makes you taboo.

- They know they shouldn't be messaging but they now want to more than ever, because you left them wanting more.

- By saying that "*it is not fair on this other guy/girl*" you paint that new person as a victim of your ex's behavior— which is unattractive. As we know, it triggers the compassion part of the mind, not the attraction part. They feel sympathy for them now and can no longer see them as equals.

What happens next?

- They may agree with you, that it isn't fair... in which case they either leave with a mirror held up to their behavior which highlights their dissatisfaction.

- Or they keep going, aware they are participating in a secret taboo conversation with a former lover.

- They may never message again. But if they don't, then they were likely never going to leave that new person anyway.

- They may push back, asking why can't we message?

- They may even try to claim you are just innocent friends now in a desperate bid to claim the moral high ground. To which you can simply explain that you both have too much chemistry or history to *ever really* just be friends. They know this is true, they're just trying to make their behavior okay. But if they are pushing back, notice how fast the tables have turned... they are fighting for you now, seeking your validation, and you are saying, 'I don't know'. Your lack of certainty puts you in the power position.

This way you leave them wanting more and they got to sample out your natural chemistry for a while. But afterwards, they have to reflect on this secret fun interaction they had with you while retreating back to this other person they're dating, which now feels like a compromise (aka. less satisfying).

Then go into No Contact and do this every time they message, making it a little longer each time, so it feels like your relationship is building momentum again. You have a fun interaction then boom— *'Wait, this is fun but it's unfair to the other guy/girl'*. Over time, this will have an attritional impact on their mind and they will start to recognize that they are not really into this new person they're seeing. And that is the goal. You do not want to date them when they are taken, you want them single.

The reason you do this is that you are now displaying that you do not need your ex. You're not begging them to leave the new person (as most would). In fact, you're actively sending them back to the very person you should be jealous of. But you're not. And this showcases that you are so unthreatened and unimpressed by this new person they are dating that you will gladly send them back to them. Most people will be so thrilled to receive any contact from their ex that they keep the chat going for as long as possible. But if you have a take it or leave it attitude, then you appear to be higher value, as you are not automatically interested, which makes your ex have to compete to earn back your attention and affection.

If they ask to meet up with you after a few fun interactions that you cut off early, you can give them an ultimatum so they break up with this new person. Or, to build momentum, start making plans to see one another in person, but then at the last stage, you can debate taking it away from them. Ponder out loud if this is even a good idea. Then they will be the ones convincing you, fighting for you. And once that is happening, you are the only priority in their mind. And that's how you transform yourself from your ex's option to a major priority.

This is a riskier decision but by being willing to risk losing them, you can turn the tables more effectively if they are susceptible to seeking your validation.

Toxic Behavior:

It is important that you always look out for yourself and avoid toxic situations. These are generally categorized as situations that make you feel manipulated, unstable, or worthless.

Sometimes the relationship itself can be toxic. This means that although you have had great times together, you mostly just bring out the worst in one another. If you are both playing games or deceiving one another or arguing non-stop, then this is a good opportunity to take time apart to question whether or not this relationship is actually healthy for you. You need to look out for yourself and your mental health first and foremost, above all possible outcomes.

Sometimes the dumper can be toxic. The warning signs here are that you feel as if they do not factor your emotional wellbeing into any of their decisions. They are selfish and rarely take responsibility for their mistakes, resulting in them never changing. They slowly pick apart at your personality, causing your sense of self-worth to diminish over time. They gaslight you, meaning they deflect blame away from themselves by causing you to question your own reality, or insisting that everything is actually your fault. It is always their way or the highway. You sometimes ask yourself, is this a relationship or a dictatorship? If you feel that you are emotionally used or abused by your ex, then you should avoid them and move on with your life. Sometimes these types of exes have troubled pasts... but just because something traumatizing has happened to them before, does not give them permission to traumatize you now.

Sometimes the dumper can be inadvertently toxic. This means that although they are likely a good person, their desires and patterns of behavior have made this situation too unhealthy for you to continue. Perhaps you are too attached to them and they are too unavailable. Perhaps they still sleep with you occasionally, but they are too uncertain about ever getting back together and keep wasting your time and damaging you emotionally. Perhaps they just want you to be friends so keep staying in contact needlessly.

It is important that you take pause and reflect on occasion. Ask yourself some tough questions you have likely been avoiding:

- Is this situation getting better or worse?

- What outcome do I want vs What outcome do I keep receiving?

- Am I rewarding bad behavior and thus incentivizing more of it?

- Are we repeating the same cycle?

- Do I need to change something fundamental about myself to make this work?

- Where is the line? What is the last straw that will make me throw in the towel?

CHAPTER 12

Reconciliation

After a period of no contact, both exes reconnect... but the road back to full reconciliation can be tricky. Dumpees usually have a lot of insecurities and anxieties since the breakup. They find it difficult to understand why the dumper is being hesitant. They think, *'Stop beating around the bush, let's just get back together already!'* But this is just the dumpee experiencing tremors from the initial rejection and trying to soothe their own anxiety, not playing to the needs of the dumper.

When meeting up with an ex, dumpees are typically very insecure about where this is going. This is understandable. They have just spent a substantial amount of time moving on with their life, letting go of their ex and healing, only to find themselves back on a possible road to reconciliation. They feel they have made so much progress in their own life that they just want the dumper to shit or get off the pot so that they can start making plans for their future one way or the other.

But dumpers are typically more avoidant and cautious when reconnecting. Sometimes they can be very direct and know exactly what they want… but that is typically in cases where the dumpee has lost interest or is moving on with someone else and the dumper is dramatically trying to stop them. Most of the time, the dumper still feels a little bit in control and as I said, don't want to feel as if they are moving backwards.

This is why there is an awkward tension between the dumper and dumpee when they first start reconnecting. They are on some level operating on different wavelengths. They may both be driving to the same destination, but they are going at different speeds, and the dumper wants the freedom to exit and turn back any time, as they worry they're going the wrong way.

This can make the dumpee feel as if this is the most high stakes first date of their life. It's barely even fun, it's just stress because they can't know if their ex is still interested or not, and they fear that if they make a romantic move on them that they may get rejected.

But what I always try to remind people is that you are now two former lovers, meeting up, alone, at night. If you walked past a bar or restaurant and saw one of your friends inside with an ex of theirs you would rightly assume something could be going on there.

This is because once that sexual door has been opened, it is always a high risk of opening again. People often cite bumper sticker slogans like, *"Once it's over, it's over"* or *"Exes are exes for a reason"*, because at the time they are saying it, they need to re-enforce that belief to themselves to shut down any hope of reconciliation so that they can move on. And that is fair enough. People do break up and not every relationship can or should be saved.

But if you want to know what someone truly believes, don't look at what they say, look at what they do.

Our society may say *"once it's over, it's over"* and we all nod with that sentiment, but we don't ever act like that's really true. Evidence? Why is it that when you are in a relationship, your current partner would not be okay with you spending time with your ex, alone? And no matter how milquetoast a "friend" you claim they are, why would any current partner not want you to invite your ex to a wedding?

Because even when you've just slept with someone once (a quick one night stand or a fling), it's now so much easier to sleep with that person again in the future. The risk of you both sleeping together again has just multiplied by ten. We all know this. It's why you are emotionally cheating if you even text your ex behind your current partner's back. Because we all know on some level, that once that door has been opened, an unspoken intimacy has been granted. And when it goes a lot further than that... when someone has touched your soul in a different way and run deep in your veins, then even if you are broken up, even if either or both of you may not want to get back together, no matter how deep you bury it, there is always going to be that unspoken chemistry; that spark, that attraction, and deep down we all know that it could be reactivated at any time with the right setting, the right moment, or the right look.

Attraction fades over time. But the sun fades every night, it doesn't mean it's gone forever. So it's important to remember that this is a former lover of yours. You aren't making a move on a married stranger who you have a little crush on. You were both in love together before. And now, they are choosing to be back in contact with you, and even willing to meet up alone. They are intentionally putting themselves in a high-risk situation. So try not to overthink this. All you need is the right mindset going in to ensure that you play to their needs and express the best version of yourself.

Subconsciously, no one wants to get with someone that considers them the best they could ever do. That suggests an imbalance of interest which communicates that you perceive yourself as lower value than the other person. Remember that your thoughts will dictate how you feel and your feelings will direct your behavior. This is why people give tells in poker. If you think too highly of your ex and worry about getting back together, then it will bleed through to your behavior. This is why you did all that work taking them off the pedestal and healing.

In a way, you are in an advantageous position with your ex as opposed to a first date. It does not feel that way, as you still have this underlying anxiety about them ever since the breakup trauma. But remember that you have the luxury of already having a built-in sexual history and natural chemistry with them.

Try to go into this with the same expectations that you would on a first or second date— *'This will be fun and let's just see what happens!'*

You don't need to think further ahead than that. Think back to any good date or even a successful one night stand you had. What were you? Present! Romance always blossoms by engaging in the present and creating a shared feeling of spontaneity.

What does the dumper need right now?

- To "try on" the relationship again without pressure

- To not feel guilty about ending things

- To have a reason to get back together

- To not feel judged

Let's take them one by one. The reason that most people fail in reconciling with their ex is because they just want to cement the commitment too soon. This means that when you meet up with your ex, you launch into a commitment renegotiation. And this is usually futile, as the dumper has no reason to reconsider getting back together yet. Why not? Because their last memory with you was likely a negative painful breakup conversation. And now based on that, you're expecting them to feel like taking the big risk of committing to you again. Notice that you would likely never think like this in any normal dating scenario. With the exception of an arranged marriage, you would never use the first date as a chance to nail down a commitment. Rather, you would let the connection grow naturally and just enjoy the moment. The dumper wants to test the waters and feel seduced back into the connection and then the commitment can follow. They do not want to feel forced into a commitment upfront with the promise that the connection may come afterwards. That's not a risk most people will want to take after time apart. They want to graduate slowly through phases; eye contact, laughing together, a kiss, then sleeping together, seeing one another again, consistency, building trust, step-by-step until commitment makes sense. Just like buying a dress in a clothing store or test-driving a new car, your ex likely wants to "try on" the relationship before purchasing. And keep in mind, you need to sample out the relationship again too. You have no idea if you really want them back unless you see how it feels to be in their company again. If you want to commit before trying the relationship on again, then you are living in the past, and this makes them feel as if they are moving backwards.

They also need to feel attraction for you again. If they feel guilty about ending the relationship because you are so hurt, then they are less likely to want to take the risk of getting back together as they will worry that you cannot emotionally handle the possibility of it failing again. Attraction requires mutual interest and respect. Don't play the victim. You are equals. How do you know if you are still playing the victim? Well, if you're still upset and locked in a cycle of asking the same confused questions from the breakup like, '*Why did you leave me*' or '*How could you do this to me*?' then that's going to be very frustrating to hear and just make them feel guilty. And that is not a recipe for reconciliation. Why? Firstly, because you're supposed to be their attractive romantic partner, not a charity case. Secondly, because you are too vulnerable. If they feel guilty, they will feel compassion for you but not attraction. This is why you need to come across as active and unphased by the breakup, as if you are at peace and can understand why things didn't work out. If you have no new insights and are still broken down, then they are likely not going to want to join you back there.

This feeds into the next point, that they need to "have a reason" to get back together. As we discussed in previous chapters, everyone likes to live within a certain story in their minds. You have your perspective, your story of the relationship and the breakup. But your ex has their own story too. If they are going to get back together with you, then they need to have a reason why this time will be different. This is why you need to somewhat agree with the breakup, not in the sense that you don't belong together, but in the sense that, in hindsight, it needed to happen because you have both benefited and grown a lot. If you have made positive changes and there is mutual understanding, with no animosity, then there is reason to believe this could actually work. This does not mean you take full responsibility for everything that went wrong and tell them they were 100% right (unless you seriously mistreated them of course). But rather, that you seem at peace and things have improved across the board. Think of it like this; when your ex's friends or family ask them what changed their mind or why you are getting back together... they likely want to have a reason that makes them sound like their original decision for breaking up was legitimate, not a foolish blunder of theirs. Don't let their ego stop them from reconsidering. Instead, let them feel like a bit of a hero who can give a justified reason why their faith has been restored in your future together. And this is what is vitally important. You are not getting *back* together, to right the wrongs of the past. You are moving forward together as two people who share compatibility.

And that feeds into the final thing your ex needs, to not feel judged. Most exes do not tell their friends or family that they are going to break no contact. Why? Because they will feel judged. They know that their friends will either ask them why they are reaching out, or tell them not to lead you on. And they likely do not consciously know exactly what they are seeking yet, they are just driven by their emotions. Asking questions like, *'Why do you want to meet up?'* beforehand or *'What was the point in messaging if we aren't getting back together?!'* afterward, is not going to help your ex to follow the natural flow of their feelings. If they have to confront their behavior, then they may get scared. If they feel you are judging their decisions, then they think others might too, so it becomes safer for them to retreat. You want your contact or time together to be a safe haven away from judgment so they can process everything and figure things out.

Just like we discussed above, when two former lovers spend time alone together, there is a higher risk of romance resurfacing. Let your ex feel free. Think about it like this. If you removed all social consequences; no friends, no family, no jobs, no culture, no social media... how would that change things?

Let's say it's years after the breakup and you decide to take a solo trip to an exotic island for some rest and relaxation. It's totally secluded, you have to get a speedboat there from an even bigger island. It's quiet and relaxing. Clear water and soft sand. You're taking a walk down the beach, and you see a figure in the distance. As they get closer, you can't believe your eyes... it's your ex. You both smile and shrug awkwardly, having been in no contact since the breakup. You ask where they're staying and they tell you that there is only one hotel on the island. On some level, you knew the answer already but you just wanted to make sure. You walk back to the hotel together and grab a drink as the sun sets. It's so quiet and peaceful. You keep talking, exchanging stories; they're living in a new city now, their work-life is chaotic just like yours. They still have that great smile and yours is reflecting right back at them. Their hair is different, but when you look into those eyes, you realize they're still the exact same. They ask you about your family and friends, they know everyone's name, it just flows so easily. They remember small intimate details that even your friends sometimes forget. You both start laughing at old inside jokes, and ordering another drink, and another one. The bar tender's face is a blur, you're just so focused on one another, as if there's a new little universe between your faces that only you both occupy. You walk them back to their hotel room door. They stop outside, look you in the eyes and say, *'This is me.'*

Ask yourself... what happens next? We all know what happens next. And that is what we are trying to capture with your ex. This is a safe haven away from judgment where your connection can naturally flow. Great relationships are formed in private together. So don't allow them to get preoccupied with other people's opinions or they may feel judged and retreat.

So when you meet up with your ex, just have fun together as if this is a first or second date. Talk in the present and future tense. Listen to their stories, laugh together, make eye contact, and if there is a romantic vibe, follow it. A lot of people get nervous about this, but as we clarified above, you are spending time with a former lover of yours. **Making a move** is not out of the ordinary for either of you. You have likely kissed this person thousands of times. Beforehand, everything has always felt natural between you both. Understandably, now it no longer feels that way (I mean you are reading a book about it, that's how unnatural it feels). But unless you have been spending a lot of time together as "just friends" then as long as you are just having a good time together, alone, with laughter, eye contact and honest conversation, it's far from a crazy idea for things to become romantic again.

If you are the woman, then create easy openings for the man to make the move for the kiss. Men like to hunt, but they also don't like complete guesswork. He should be the one to officially make the move. Firstly, so he can feel as if he took a little risk and it paid off. Men like that validation. Secondly, so he also has to consciously make some physical effort. And thirdly, because if you make the move then you serve yourself up on a platter to him and he may get "casual" vibes from you. You can't make it too easy for him or he may feel he achieved his goal so fast that he should just move onto the next one.

If you are the man, make small gestures first like a flirty comment or light hand or leg touching. You always need to read the room and test their temperature. Calculated risks. Assuming that is all going fine then you are likely safe to go for the kiss once a good opportunity emerges. If for whatever reason she pulls away or says no, stay calm. She may just have a mental block holding her back, or is not currently interested. Either way, do not start apologizing. The moment you apologize then the kiss is off the table for the rest of the night. It also makes things awkward. Instead, act almost amused. Just own it! Be composed and unbroken, even smile, and respond something like, *'I was always going to do that, it's us, it's what we do'* or if she seemed highly interested beforehand, *'We both knew I was going to do that because we both want to.'* You would be surprised how confidence and suggestion can win most people over, especially if they are already susceptible to it. When a risk is being taken between two people, there is a chaotic force and a stable force. The stable force is more in tune with reality and is interpreted as sane and therefore safe. If you stay upbeat and unphased, she is more likely to join your wavelength as it seems stable and therefore safe, whereas if you break down into tears or apologize then you are playing the chaotic role, as you are admitting to being wrong and now seem out of place in reality. Therefore she is right to stop you, as you are making her play the stable role. As long as you don't break and seem unphased by a brief rejection then the kiss is still on the table for every minute you remain in one another's company.

But sometimes it doesn't go so smoothly. Just because you want to be present and avoid talking about the breakup, does not mean your ex won't. They may have pressing concerns or want to resolve issues fast. Fine. At some point, you are going to have to talk about what happened. How you **talk about the breakup** matters. Most people make the mistake of launching into their own feelings and even ranting at their ex. This is natural because they have been stressed, and have so many thoughts about the breakup that talking about it can feel like releasing a pressure valve. Sadly, this may put your ex off as it reveals you are still hung up about the past (meaning you are playing the victim) or it exposes how overly invested you still are.

Instead, vibe it out. Play it safe by listening more than you speak initially. This way you listen to understand, not just to respond. This is the difference between a conversation and a disagreement. You are on the same team, not at war with one another.

Let them lead this conversation so you can see where their head is at. We want this to be a healthy and effective communication, which involves listening to what they have to say and not getting defensive. When we get defensive, we are just canceling out the other person's offense, but we do not actually listen. A clear example of this would be if your ex or even your current partner says, *'you're always working late I never get to see you,'* and you respond with, *'I have to work late, what do you want me to do — lose my job!? Besides, you're always out with your friends anyway!'*

By getting defensive, you miss the woods for the trees and fail to see what is really being communicated. They miss you and want more time with you. But instead of facing that reality, you are refusing to hear that complaint, justifying your time spent away from them, and attacking how they spend their free time. This is not an effective communication that will lead to reconciliation.

This is what is wrong with just being defensive and not staying composed. If you do not absorb the information and find a way to empathize with where they're coming from, then you will both walk away angry or upset, but with no real understanding of one another. Instead, if your ex is going to explain how they feel now, or what they think was wrong with your relationship, listen to why, without interrupting them. When they finish, you can reiterate some of their reasons back to them so they can see that you get it. Example: *'Oh... so you think A because B?'* Ex: *'Yes, and A and B makes me feel C.'*

Now you understand what they think and feel. Assume that their position is fair and balanced. Now you can respond with your own, *'I see. I thought A because D, and that made me feel Y.'* Choosing to listen first allows you to detect the tone of conversation and then follow their lead.

You also set a good example of how the communication should go by being respectful and listening. You then have the luxury of incorporating their answer into your own, making it seem like you are both really on the same page.

It can be tough having an open and honest conversation and sharing blame. Even if you do not get what you want right away, as long as you stay composed and are open and honest with one another, then you at least communicate effectively and can both walk away from the exchange with an understanding of eachother, which is a big positive, because it proves you can actually work together and that difficult conversations can be easy, which is a breadcrumb for future reconciliation.

Sometimes it can be tough to communicate effectively with our ex because we are still holding onto some anger and resentment about their decision to break up with us or for their poor behavior within the relationship. This is very normal. But if you do want to reconcile, it is important to ***forgive*** them if possible. This does not mean that you just forgive toxic behavior like cheating or lying as if it was nothing, but during your time apart, you should have taken a step back from the impressionist painting that is your relationship and gained some clarity about what role both of you played in this relationship and why.

Despite what you may have felt about them while your passionate romance endured, your ex is just a flawed human who bounces from mistake to mistake just like the rest of us. They have morning breath, insecurities, childhood issues, anxieties about their own identity and uncertainties about their future. They're human.

They made the choice to walk away from you because at the time that was one of the only decisions they felt they could make. This original sin may feel somewhat unforgivable to you because they chose to leave out of their own free will. But does free will even really exist? In many ways, we are bound by the restrictions of our imagination, our experience, and our limited information at the time. All of these factors cause us to make each and every decision. In essence, we are only as free to choose out of the options we can already think of.

Your ex had many reasons for ending the relationship that they likely struggle to articulate fully as it was a feeling. They may have been uncertain about where their life was going, who they were, where they should live, what they should be doing as a career, or battling undiagnosed anxiety and depression. You never know what someone else is going through, and they often struggle to contextualize it themselves.

For this reason, you should forgive your ex for making this mistake. They chose to break up with you and risked losing you forever. But remember that in the process of doing so they hurt themselves too. Now after time apart they are uncertain about their decision, just like they were at the time of the breakup.

Similar to how you made mistakes in the relationship or during and after the breakup that you wish you could take back, they have made mistakes by even inflicting the breakup upon both of you in the first place. By reaching out they are on some level acknowledging that mistake. They are physically acting out to correct a mistake.

So despite what you or your ego may think, you can forgive this person. They did what they thought was right at the time, and now they are doing that again, but in your favor. If you cannot forgive mistakes, then you don't allow yourself to make any either, and that way we all remain stagnant and terrified of risk. Forgive their mistakes just as you should forgive your own. Accept that the past is done, it's written, it cannot be changed. But you can both influence the present, which will help you to build a bright future together. So try to forgive them for what they did 'then', and accept that all we have is now.

Once you have met up with your ex, discussed your problems, forgiven them and yourself, and romance has blossomed, then you are on the right path back to healthy reconciliation. At first, it may feel as if things are not quite the same between you both. Most people chalk this up to the ***trust*** being broken. And that is fair, trust has to be earned. But remember that by staying in relatively consistent contact, showing up to dates and making sacrifices, you are both making these little promises to one another and then fulfilling them. This is what naturally solidifies trust over time.

You may still wonder about officially becoming a couple again. Ideally, this will be the dumper's suggestion. After all, they were the ones to leave, so they should be the ones to return and recommit.

But life is not always ideal. If you have been seeing one another for two months and there is no mention of being in a relationship, then you may start to worry you are merely Friends with Benefits. This is an understandable fear to have. Your ex may just be avoidant and not want to mention the elephant in the room (your relationship). If this is the case, you may have to be the brave one to bring it up. But as always, taking calculated risks is the best way forward. Rather than sitting them down for a serious discussion, you should subtly start nudging them in the right direction.

If you're in bed together or having coffee one morning, you should invite them to a public event where friends or family will be. Maybe it's a birthday party, or a work event, something somewhere public where your ex will have to be seen with you, which means others will become consciously aware that you are together again. Watch their face closely after you invite them. If they have a slight look of panic and then quickly find an excuse, then they may not be on the path towards officially getting back together. If this continues or you notice them pull further away, then you should be the one to end it this time, explaining that you want to move forwards and you get the impression they want to move backwards. If they don't push back at all, then you are right to leave them.

But if they say yes to dating you publicly, then you will feel more secure and they will slowly start to evolve back into viewing this as a real relationship with a future, as you are now both fulfilling those roles publicly.

But if you find yourself just dating your ex occasionally, or are uncertain about your status as a lover or a friend, or you want to **nail down a commitment**, then you may need to just bite the bullet and sit down and talk about this. If so, always make sure that you are not pitching yourself to them.

It's a small but important linguistic trick. Let's say you sit down across from someone and you say, '*I have really strong feelings for you. When I was next to you in bed, I was thinking about how much I like you. I really want this to go somewhere. I find you very funny and I think you are so beautiful. I want us to be a couple. What do you say?*'

That is a lovely sentiment, but you are framing the relationship in the singular (I). *'I have feelings for you. I think you are beautiful!'*— this all sounds solitary and one-sided. Most people do not realize they do this, but by isolating their feelings and emotions, they are communicating as if they are in anticipation of rejection. This makes it sound like you are pitching yourself to your boss, not your equal.

Instead, always talk as if you both are already an item, a foregone conclusion. *'We have such a good time together, we laugh non-stop, everyone is jealous of our connection. When we were in bed together the other day, it just felt obvious we belong together officially. What do you think?'*

This way you frame it in such a way that they are almost forced to view themselves as already on your team and you are pointing to your joint experiences together, as opposed to describing what it feels like to be in your mind experiencing their amazing aura, as if they are some sort of celebrity you admire. This puts you on equal footing with your partner because you are describing them as if they are already your partner. This makes them feel as if they have already been in a relationship with you for some time, so why not make it official. As opposed to placing them in this power position above you, hearing your pitch, but ultimately getting to make the final call on whether or not this is good enough.

Once you've reconciled and are back together, you both need to take the lessons from the breakup and avoid repeating the same mistakes. If the same patterns emerge time and time again then perhaps you are both just incompatible long-term. Maintaining a healthy relationship over a long period of time can be difficult but rewarding. It requires honest communication, a lot of laughter, space to maintain independent interests, sacrifice, teamwork, great sex, new experiences, but also a bedrock of consistency and reliability, financial stability and forward planning.

Reconciliation is a step-by-step process. Sometimes it's fast and clear, other times it's a slow winding road. But try not to be too outcome orientated. Just like dating, the experience is everything. So be present and just enjoy the ride for what it is.

Final Reflections

Breakups are a painful, confusing process. They often leave us feeling abandoned, unattractive, worthless, raw and shell-shocked. But it is important to remind yourself that you were strong enough to live an amazing life before you even began this relationship. You were even attractive enough to seduce your ex in the first place. So whether you think so or not, you will get through this, you will love again, and you will continue to progress forward.

At this moment, there is an endless list of exciting opportunities ahead of you. Maybe you're ready to tackle them all. Maybe you're still solely focused on the breakup and hope to reconcile with your ex. And that's okay too. But you don't need this person. You're telling yourself you need them in order to justify wanting them back. But you know deep down, you don't need them.

And this is why you have to make peace with your biggest fear. You need to forgive your ex even if they don't come back. If they never reach out. If they never want to reconcile. Just like you need to forgive yourself, you need to forgive them too. Because they are just as flawed as anyone else. And for whatever reason and the current circumstances in their life, they don't feel they can or should reach out. We can't know why they feel that way or what they are doing, but due to their life experience, and the limitations of their own knowledge or imagination, they can't bring themselves to come back.

And that's okay.

Because while they feel that way, they aren't worth your time either. So they are doing you a favor and not wasting your current, present tense time. They believe they are doing the right thing for them, and for you, by not coming back. And maybe they are wrong, in which case they are making a mistake and you can forgive them because they are just human and they make mistakes. But maybe they are right… in which case they are doing what's best for you too.

So what feels like a cold act of selfishness and defiance against you, is likely not perceived or intended that way by them. Therefore, you should forgive them, as they likely are trying their best to do the right thing in this crazy adventure we call life.

Even if they are wrong, we forgive them, not to relieve them of the burden of our judgment, but for ourselves. Because as the saying goes, *'holding onto anger is like drinking poison in the hopes your enemy will die from it.'*

In the end, you will make your own decisions and what to do in your breakup situation. All I can do is share my knowledge and experience from the patterns I have seen over the years. I hope this book brings you what you think you need. Sometimes after a breakup, we lose faith in ourselves, or we lose faith in love itself. You may never want to risk loving again. But that feeling is temporary and being broken-hearted after a breakup is not a sign of someone who should avoid love. That's a sign of someone who knows how to love, who soaks it up for what it's worth, and appreciates its real value.

There are times, especially in the anger stage of your grief, that you may decide to blame men or blame women. It's ironic in a way, that a breakup can hurt us so much that we lose faith in something as big as a concept (like love itself)... but we keep faith in the person who made us lose it. We may blame women or men, but we won't allow ourselves to truly blame that one person (our ex). We like to think they're perfect and if they return then our faith in love will be restored.

But don't forget that you choose how you see the world. You may walk down busy city streets and just feel tired, defeated and empty. A sea of blurred faces pass by in a monotonous crowd. But amongst that crowd of strangers, you previously found someone you truly valued. And if you are open to it, you may find another, and another, and another.

Through answering thousands of emails from people in different cultures, continents, and walks of life, I have seen that despite what our most cynical side may like to think, there are a lot of great people out there. And they all want the same thing. They all feel the same way. Although navigating your way through an agonizing breakup or through the precarious dating scene can be tough, I would implore you not to give up or check out. Don't willfully blind yourself just because things got so dark that it became hard to see.

Just like you started this book knowing it would take time to complete, healing from your breakup will take time too. But notice that you likely felt a little different when you read page one, compared to how you feel now. You may feel a little fresher, a little more prepared, a little more understood, a little more informed, a little more optimistic. And if you can already notice the difference in your own progress in the time it took to read this book, then you know that there is not only light at the end of the tunnel... but a bright future ahead.

So don't worry... you're going to be fine.

Acknowledgments

My clients, subscribers and viewers who have bravely shared their stories, experiences and thoughts on this topic since 2017, and without whom, this book would not exist.

Notes

1. William Shakespeare, '*As you Like it*', Act II Scene VII Line 138, *1623*.

2. Michael Lynn, '*Scarcity Effects on Value: A Quantitative Review of the Commodity Theory Literature*', *1991*

3. https://onlinedoctor.superdrug.com/the-one-that-got-away/

4. Paul T Costa, Jeffrey H. Herbst, Robert R McCrae, Ilene C. Siegler, '*Personality at Midlife: Stability, Intrinsic Maturation, and Response to Life Events*', Dec 1, 2000. https://doi.org/10.1177/107319110000700405

5. Erin R. Whitchurch, Timothy D. Wilson, Daniel T. Gilbert, *"He Loves Me, He Loves Me Not . . . ": Uncertainty Can Increase Romantic Attraction*. Dec 17 2010. https://doi.org/10.1177/0956797610393745

6. Helen E. Fisher, Lucy L. Brown, Arthur Aron, Greg Strong, and Debra Mashek, '*Reward, Addiction, and Emotion Regulation Systems Associated With Rejection in Love*', 01 July 2010

7. Tech.co, Conor Cawley, '*Flirt, Fake, Make Them Wait – The Truth About How We Treat Each Other Online*', Oct 19 2018. https://tech.co/news/flirt-fake-wait-treat-people-online-2018-10

8. https://onlinedoctor.superdrug.com/is-it-stalking/

Printed in Great Britain
by Amazon